ELEMENTS OF LIBERTARIAN LEADERSHIP

Notes on the theory, methods,
and practice of freedom

BY LEONARD E. READ

The Foundation for Economic Education, Inc.
Irvington-on-Hudson, New York   1962

The Author and Publisher

Leonard E. Read, author of *Conscience of the Majority, Government—An Ideal Concept, Miracle of the Market, Students of Liberty, Why Not Try Freedom?*, and other books and articles, is President of the Foundation for Economic Education, organized in 1946.

The Foundation is an educational champion of private ownership, the free market, the profit and loss system, and limited government. It is nonprofit and nonpolitical. Sample copies of the Foundation's monthly study journal, THE FREEMAN, are available on request.

PUBLISHED MARCH 1962

CONTENTS

FOREWORD

IT IS DIFFICULT even to set forth the libertarian ideal, but expounding it is simple compared to living by it. Nonetheless, life lived according to right principles can never be more than sporadic except as the ideal is sought for, held up, and used as a guide.

I have no reason for attempting a manual of libertarian leadership except the conviction—born of three decades of trial and error—that our waning individual liberty is more difficult to restore than most people judge. It would be shameful for any person, thinking he knows how deep the ore lies, to keep silent while millions of people wastefully prospect on the surface.

First, a word about terms. I use *freedom* and *liberty* as synonyms, that is, interchangeably. A case has been made for ascribing different values to these terms but the distinction, if any, is never generally understood and, thus, is more or less useless for communicative purposes.

The term *libertarian* is used because nothing better has been found to replace *liberal,* a term that has been most successfully appropriated by contemporary authoritarians. As long as *liberal* meant liberation from the authoritarian state, it was a handy and useful generalization. It has come to mean little more than state liberality with other people's money.

Next, the solution to the problem of rescuing an individual liberty on the skids requires, broadly speaking, the mastery of two disciplines: the *philosophy of freedom* and the *methodology of freedom*. The former has to do with an understanding of what freedom actually is, and the latter with the techniques, means, and methods by which an improved state of freedom may be effected.

The emphasis in this volume is on methodology. Assuming an individual has mastered the philosophical aspects of freedom, what can he do about it? With whom does he work? What are his limitations? His potentialities?

Methodology must not be sold short. Indeed, if everyone—freedom devotees and their opposites—had his method right, there would be no real philosophical problem. Right method, according to this thesis, consists of self-improvement. If everyone were devoted to the perfection of self, there could be no meddlers amongst us, and without meddlers there could be no socialism.

Of course, philosophy and methodology cannot be compartmented, entirely. To be a master of liberty's rationale one must, to be consistent, behave in a libertarian manner. One cannot, for instance, stand truly for liberty and regard as villains or fools those who disagree, without qualifying as an intellectual authoritarian!

So, throughout this volume there will be traces of

philosophy for, without some of it, the methods would be attached to no purpose. Perhaps to establish an author-reader understanding at the outset, an important philosophical definition is in order:

Liberty, like *laissez faire,* is often thought of as synonymous with unrestrained action. The thought is incorrect as related to both terms. Liberty, for instance, does not and cannot include any action, regardless of sponsorship, which lessens the liberty of a single human being. To argue contrarily is to claim that liberty can be composed of liberty negations. Patently absurd! Unrestraint carried to the point of impairing the liberty of others is the exercise of license, not liberty. To minimize the exercise of license is to maximize the area of liberty. Ideally, government would restrain license, not indulge in it; make it difficult, not easy; disgraceful, not popular. A government that does otherwise is licentious, not libertarian.

Finally, this volume contains little that is new, except the arrangement. Most of the material has appeared over the past five years in books and pamphlets, some of it in *The Freeman* and *Notes from FEE,* publications of The Foundation for Economic Education, Inc. This is an attempt to organize the numerous materials into a single, usable manual for those who would give liberty a hand.

                                        L. E. R.

CHAPTER 1

FAITH AND FREEDOM

ALMOST EVERYONE says he favors freedom; just try to find a single individual who says he does not. The search would almost certainly prove fruitless. Indeed, so many declare themselves for freedom and against communism that hundreds of organizations now exist to satisfy the common devotion to this attractive term. But, in spite of this lip service to freedom, our actual liberties continue to dwindle. The centralized state makes more and more of our decisions for us.

Why is it that the millions of us who vocally proclaim for freedom do not constitute a solid front against the omnipotent state? Perhaps it is because some who proclaim their devotion to freedom do not understand the requirements of freedom, its "operational imperatives." Thomas à Kempis, the fourteenth century author of *The Imitation of Christ*, saw the problem of peace in similar terms. "Many favor peace," he wrote, "but not many favor the things that make for peace." When it comes

---

* This chapter is from an address, "Endowed by Their Creator," delivered as The Mayflower Lecture on May 7, 1961, at the Mayflower Community Congregational Church, Oklahoma City.

to an understanding of the proper means and methods for achieving the goal of freedom, there are some real divisions among those who say they believe in freedom. Why is this so?

When speaking of believers in freedom, I do not refer —for the purpose of this inquiry—to those Americans who have a distaste for the godless apparatus headquartering in Moscow. That would be nearly all of us. Nor do I have in mind all who avow a dislike for state socialism. Or, the millions who give lip service to "the American way of life."

When I speak of the differences of opinion in the freedom camp, I am referring to the relatively few of us— tens of thousands, not millions—who claim an affinity for libertarian ideals. When the inquiry is thus brought into focus, the question reads, "Why do we—the hard core of the free market, private property, limited government philosophy—disagree with each other? Why do *we* not present a solid front? For it must be acknowledged that even we have pronounced differences of opinions and that we are in constant argument with each other. Why? That's the question.

A Dying Movement?

Several years ago I put this puzzle to a distinguished American conservative who, at the time, was being taken to task by scholarly individuals who shared, in a general way, his own ideological persuasions. His answer—no doubt somewhat influenced by pique—was, "This fight-

ing among ourselves is the sign of a dying movement."
Let us hope that he was wrong for, if not, the cause of
freedom would be hopeless, so vigorous are the arguments among the few of us we call, "We."

I shall try to make the case for a contrary interpreta-
tion: These sharp differences of opinion among those of
us who in a general way share libertarian ideals are the
sign of a movement not yet come fully alive, of a movement suffering birth pains.

However, before going further, it is necessary that we
understand what these arguments among ourselves are
really about. Can they be reduced to a single issue? In
the first place, they are not about the desirability of
freedom, for we are all agreed on that. Nor, except
in a few isolated instances, do they revolve around the
question of anarchy, or no government at all, versus limited government. All but a few freedom devotees believe
in limited government, that is, a formal, legal agency of
society which invokes a common justice, and secures the
rights of all men by restricting such destructive actions
as fraud, violence, and predation.

What Price Freedom?

What, then, is the nature of the contentions so rife
among us? The arguments, stripped of all their semantic
inaccuracies, boil down to: *How cheaply can freedom
be bought?*—although it is rarely so stated. Is freedom
something that can be had for the wishing? For casual
effort? Is it a prize to be won by delegating the chore to

some hired hands? Or, is the price of freedom an intellectual and spiritual renaissance with all the hard thinking and difficult introspection required to energize such
a revolution in thinking?

Some believe that freedom can be had simply by un-
covering card-carrying communists and then calling
them names. To these people, our ills originate in Moscow. Be done with Soviet agents and, presto, freedom!

Others believe that the loss of freedom stems from
what they call "the ignorant masses." Merely finance
educational programs aimed at "selling the man in the
street." Teach this ignoramus that there is no such thing
as a free lunch or some other such simplicity that can
be grasped as he passes a bulletin board or drowsily reads
baby talk literature in a barber's chair. Gain freedom
by writing a check!

A considerable number offer political action as their
highest bid for freedom. Organize "right down to the
precinct level" and elect "the right people" to public
office. As if freedom could be had by activating the present absence of understanding, so as to shift existing ignorance into high gear!

Another group believes that the price need be no
higher than the cost of beaming radio reports behind the
Iron Curtain—relating to those slave peoples how lux-
uriously we Americans revel in our gadgetry. Freedom
as a consequence of exciting international envy!

Then there are those who would insure "a free world"
by having the federal government coercively take the

fruits of our own labor to subsidize foreign governments. As if friendship could be purchased for an exchange of cash; as if subsidized relationships were the essence of freedom; as if this kind of communism at home would discourage world communism!

The highest priced bid, in dollar terms, is the resort to the sword. Outdo the godless states in the hardware of mass slaughter and American freedom will remain intact!

Preservation—or Restoration?

But it is useless to name all the various panaceas proffered as our bids for freedom—bids aimed at the mere preservation of individual freedom. For we cannot preserve that which has already been so largely lost. We have a restoration job on our hands. Freedom must experience a rebirth in America; that is, we must re-establish it from fundamental principles. Most of the bids aimed at a renewed freedom are far too low. If this were not a fact, freedom would have been restored by now. Indeed, it would never have been lost. The price of freedom is not increased political activity or even economic understanding, nor can the cost of freedom be stated in dollar terms.

Political collectivism, the antithesis of individual freedom, can be likened to a cancer. It is not like a skin cancer that can be treated with relative ease; it resembles the type known as "metastasis"—the wildly spreading kind. The disease has spread through the whole body politic, a fact not likely to be observed except by those

who work full time on behalf of freedom. Nothing short
of the best therapy ever known to man can cope with
this problem.[1]

Freedom To Become What?

Libertarian leadership depends on finding an answer
to the question: *What is man's earthly purpose?* Acknowledged, no two of us can reach precisely similar answers.
Nonetheless, the quest and the finding of an answer
satisfactory to each of us—this intellectual and spiritual
effort—is a part of the price we must pay for freedom.
Without a purpose in life, a fundamental datum line,
a basic point of reference, no effort aimed at restoring
freedom makes much sense. Man needs to be free in
order that he may fulfill the demands of his nature.
Freedom to become what? is the only relevant question.

My own answer to this question will be given and
explained in the next chapter, but here let me refer
to the two categories of freedom, inner and outer, psychological and sociological—each area subject to freedom
impairments. Sociological restraints have to do with man
imposing his will by force on other men—authoritarianism of one kind or another.

The psychological restraints on freedom, on the other
hand, are such things as ignorance, insensitivity, pride,
stupidity, personality defects, and the like. They are, no

---

[1] "It is not a hazarded assertion, it is a great truth, that once
things are gone out of their ordinary course, it is by acts out of
the ordinary course they can alone be re-established."—Edmund
Burke in a letter to William Elliott, Esq., 1795.

doubt, more stubborn impediments to emergence than are the sociological restraints. They might be termed spiritual faults which demand a spiritual remedy. This aspect of the problem is beyond my competence and outside the scope of this manual. It is enough for me to touch on only a narrow but extremely important phase of the sociological aspect; man's inhumanity to man as manifested by the misuse of governmental power.

Spiritual, Political, and Economic

This brings us to the second part of the over-all price that must be paid for freedom: the intellectual and spiritual effort required to grasp the full implications of the idea expressed in these words of the Declaration of Independence: [Men] . . . "are endowed by their Creator with certain unalienable rights; that among these are life, liberty, and the pursuit of happiness. . . ." This, quite obviously, is a political concept with tremendous spiritual overtones. Indeed, this concept is at once spiritual, political, and economic. It is spiritual in proclaiming the Creator as the endower of men's rights and, thus, as sovereign. It is political in the sense that such an acknowledgment implicitly denies the state as the endower of men's rights and, thus, the state is not sovereign. And this is an economic concept because it follows from a man's inherent right to life that he has a right to sustain his life, the sustenance of life being nothing more nor less than the fruits of one's own labor.

As freedom is a necessary part of godliness, so is spiritual faith—godliness—a necessary part of freedom. Or,
so runs my argument. Freedom is to be restored only as
we place faith in our Creator, and such faith is possible
only as the human spirit is freed of stifling restraints.
Spiritual faith and freedom are thus two *reciprocating*
parts of a Divine Principle. In a strict sense, they are inseparable and, thus, they tend to rise and fall together.
I use the word "tend" simply because they are not inseparable as are two sides of a coin, but inseparable
as are two mountain climbers securely tied to each
other by a long rope. There is a "play" between
them, and it is this "play" which permits one to help
the other advance and which may keep the other from
falling. In any final analysis, they do rise and fall together. Alexis de Tocqueville had a full appreciation of
this point:

> For my own part, I doubt that man can ever support
> at the same time complete religious independence [atheism
> or agnosticism] and entire political freedom. And I am
> inclined to think that if faith be wanting in him, he
> must be subject; and if he be free, he must believe.[2]

Unless we believe that man's rights are endowments
of our Creator and, therefore, inalienable, we must conclude that the rights to life and liberty derive from some
human collective and that they are alienable, being at
the disposal of the collective will. There is no third al-

---

[2] From *Democracy in America* (New York: Alfred A. Knopf,
1945), p. 22.

ternative; we *believe* in the one or we *submit* to the other. If the latter, there is no freedom in the social sense; there is despotism.

If we lack this spiritual faith, our rights to life and liberty are placed on the altar of collective caprice and they must suffer whatever fate the political apparatus dictates. The record clearly shows what this fate is. Russia is the most degraded example, but practically every other nation, including our own, drifts in Russia's direction. Among the Russians we note that freedom of choice has been forcibly lifted from the individual and shifted to the political collective. The dictator and his henchmen prescribe the manner in which the fruits of the citizen's labor shall be expended and how his life shall be lived.

Two Parts of a Divine Principle

There is one other feature of the Moscow apparatus about which we should become acutely conscious: its godlessness. This is no accident. The political collective would undermine its own power if it condoned the peoples' belief in the Creator as the endower of man's rights. If Russians believed in and understood the full implications of the Creator concept, the political collective would fall. As suggested above, freedom and spiritual faith are two parts of a Divine Principle and tend to rise and fall together.

We do not have to confine our observations to Russia, however, to see faithlessness and the loss of freedom going hand in hand. This same phenomenon can readily be seen here at home. While we cannot measure the loss of spiritual faith with anywhere near the precision that we can calculate the loss of freedom, there is a great deal of evidence to support the conclusion that they are falling or, shall we say, failing together. For instance, we can measure with a near precision the average citizen's loss in freedom of choice as it relates to the fruits of his own labor. During the past twelve decades, by reason of governmental expansion, his freedom of choice has declined steadily from 95-98 per cent to about 65 per cent— and the trend grows apace. In other words, taxation which once took only 2-5 per cent of earned income now deprives us of about 35 per cent.

A Diminishing Faith

Let us now reflect on the loss of faith in the Creator as the endower of man's rights. This spiritual concept is rarely mentioned in our day. For all practical purposes, it is a forgotten element of faith. I am unaware of any contemporary textbook which develops the implications of this concept. Permit me to make an even more serious charge: The Creator sovereignty concept issues from all too few American pulpits! Bear in mind that the American ideal of individual liberty and limited government is the political implementation of a religious concept of man. Early American clergymen deserve much of the credit for this magnificent accomplishment. But their successors, by and large, and especially the men who have gained access to the ecclesiastical sounding boards, have forsaken this path and are now following in other footsteps. As a consequence, most of the people of our country have already crossed the border and have left this spiritual concept to history. They have accepted new ideas which put their God-given rights at the mercy of the state, which is, by its nature, an amoral and, thus, a godless apparatus.[3] Here at home we sadly note another proof that faithlessness and the loss of freedom fail and fall together.

The Ultimate Goal

I do not mean to suggest that we should turn from the godless state to the Creator concept for reasons of mere material advantage. That would be to pervert religion, to get the sequence upside down, to confuse cause and effect. Faith in Infinite Consciousness—our Creator —is a spiritual achievement, a goal for which one strives for its own sake. The goal is the emergence of the individual human spirit that it may achieve its fullest measure of immortality. Desirable earthly consequences are a by-product of this pursuit. The highest aim is to bring individual consciousness into as near a harmony as possible with Infinite Consciousness.

However, once we have the sequence right, which is

---

[3] For an explanation of the amorality of the state, see my "Conscience of the Majority," *The Freeman*, March 1961 (The Foundation for Economic Education, Irvington-on-Hudson, N. Y.). Copy on request.

to say, when we first focus our thoughts and energies on
life's highest purpose, there follow the most efficacious
earthly consequences. It is only when we tap The Source
of all blessings that blessings become the lot of mankind. "Seek ye first the Kingdom of God and all these
things shall be added unto you."

The Foundations of Limited Government

As the removal of restraints—the practice of freedom
—releases the perceptive powers of the individual and
permits spirituality to grow, so does faith in the Creator
bestow an increasing freedom. As suggested earlier, no
governmental apparatus can lord it over a people who
conceive of their rights as deriving from their Creator.
This conception makes impossible, among those who
hold it, any ascendancy of government beyond its prin-
cipled position. It restricts the powers of government to
the exercise of such force as any individual is morally
warranted in employing. The individual, as a being responsible to his Creator, has a moral right to defend his
own life and liberty and property against fraud, violence,
misrepresentation, and predation. Lacking this right, he
could not discharge his responsibility for the proper stew-
ardship of his own life. Government, logically, can have
no powers beyond those which individuals may properly
exercise—if the Creator concept be accepted. Man is free
to act creatively or productively as he pleases. Here we
have the absence of any and all political restraints on

creative action, in short, total freedom from governmental interference in this area.

I have used the term "total freedom." It must be understood that freedom does not and cannot include actions which impair another's freedom. Freedom, except in its psychological sense, is a social term. Socially speaking, freedom has a place in our vocabulary only as it describes a felicitous relationship of man to man. Therefore, freedom is not and cannot be synonymous with unrestrained action. To do as one pleases, if it infringes upon the freedom of another, is not freedom at all—it's tyranny. It is impossible for freedom to be composed of freedom negations. Total freedom, then, as relating to society and government, is the ideal to be sought. This is a goal to be kept uppermost in mind, and any deviations from it are to be disapproved.

The Power of Right Thinking

At this juncture, there is one other point that needs emphasis: Merely to agree with the spiritual concept that men are endowed by their Creator with the rights to life and liberty is not at all adequate for bringing about the renaissance our serious national situation requires. Many people give lip service to this concept without relating the concept to its practical, political application. All of its implications must be brought into sharp focus in the minds of each of us. If this be accomplished —and it takes a bit of doing—then government, in our ideal theory, is automatically excluded from any action beyond securing the rights with which we are endowed by our Creator. Governmental tampering with or management of any creative activity becomes unthinkable. Creative activity is a manifestation of the Creator as it shows forth in men and, in good conscience, is not to be hampered or restrained or destroyed by man or any of his organizations. To interfere with this Divine Energy in any manner whatsoever is to thwart and defy our Creator. It is man putting himself above God.

Once enough of us to compose a leadership—it need not be large—accept and understand the full implications of "endowed by their Creator"; once we have our fundamental principles straight; once we have brought ourselves into harmony with Divine Providence; once we conquer completely any impulses to dethrone the Creator; then, our social problems untangle and the way to individual growth, evolution, emergence becomes clear. Life and liberty unobstructed by man, yes! But there is more, for in seeking to realize life's highest purpose lies the pursuit of happiness. We are truly happy only when we are in a perpetual state of hatching, our own consciousness opening to Infinite Consciousness.[4]

---

[4] "There was a Greek philosopher, Heraclitus, who lived five centuries before Christ. Change is the law of life, he wrote, everything is in flux—including man. We are creatures in transit. We can't drift along as we are, just being our jolly little selves; we must grow, and if we don't, we decay. Heraclitus put this in a colorful way when he said: 'We are here as in an egg.' Now an egg cannot go on and on just being a good egg; it must either hatch or go bad. This is the nature of an egg, and in this respect the demand of our own nature is not essentially different."—From *The Freeman,* July 1960, p. 53.

The Flow of Creative Energy .

Let us now reflect on the way of life that naturally follows an application of the endowed-by-their-Creator concept. We need only take note of several seemingly self-evident facts.

The most striking fact is that the creative potentiality in any individual is unknown. We only know that the aggregate potentialities among all who live is enormous; that creation manifests itself in strange ways and through persons we have no manner of guessing. For instance, about a century ago, there was a twelve-year-old lad of humble origin, a railroad newsboy, whom a trainman picked up by the ears and pulled into the baggage car. Who could have guessed that this boy would become the world's greatest inventor? Little did that trainman know that he was dealing with Thomas Alva Edison through whom Creative Energy was to flow with practical consequences rarely if ever equaled.

All energy seeks its destination, the fulfillment of its purpose. Holes in the dikes are but the result of potential energy trying to become flowing, kinetic energy. Likewise, Infinite Consciousness, at least as I conceive it, tries to flow into and through persons, manifesting itself as individual human consciousness. When not too much obstructed, it shows forth in man as insight, cognition, inspiration, inventiveness, in short, creativeness. Some creativeness we classify as material, other as intellectual, but all creativeness is spiritual.

Through whom will this Creative Energy flow? We can

never know in advance any more than we can know what form it will take.

We do know that it manifests itself more or less to some extent in nearly everyone. For, who has never had an idea? We also know that the consciousness of a few is greatly expanded when compared to the mill run of us, as in an Edison, a Goethe, a Milton, a Beethoven, a Leonardo da Vinci, or a Henri Poincare, to mention but a few. Further, we know that it never manifests itself in any two individuals identically. Indeed, it is infinitely varied in its manifestations. Picture it as waves of energy, as an electrical current, sometimes imperceptible, now and then—and perhaps only momentarily—strong and vibrant. It shows forth unequally, differently, infinitely throughout humankind.

The Law of Attraction

These infinitely varied waves of Creative Energy have their source in Infinite Consciousness and, accordingly, are governed by the laws thereof. These laws we try to discern and, to the extent that we do, we grow in consciousness, that is, partake of Infinite Consciousness. One law or principle, as stated by an eminent scientist, is highly relevant to this thesis:

> All the phenomena of astronomy, which had baffled the acutest minds since the dawn of history, the movement of the heavens, of the sun and the moon, the very complex movement of the planets, suddenly tumble to-

gether and become intelligible in terms of the one stag-
gering assumption, this mysterious "attractive force." And
not only the movements of the heavenly bodies, far more
than that, the movements of earthly bodies, too, are seen
to be subject to the same mathematically definable law,
instead of being, as they were for all previous philosophers,
mere unpredictable happen-so's.[5]

Why is the above quotation so relevant to this thesis?
Simply because all the highly varied creative energies,
as they manifest themselves in millions of individuals
the world over, fall under this very law, this mysterious
attractive force. *These creative energies have an affinity
for each other and, if not impeded, that is, if free, will
automatically, spontaneously, miraculously configurate
or draw together in the most unpredictable patterns to
form the goods and services men live by.* Think of yourself. Reflect on how helpless you would be were your life
dependent on the tiny consciousness which is yours. You
would perish. So would anyone else, similarly handi-
capped. Yet, we all live in relative luxury. What accounts
for this? It cannot be explained except in terms of creative energy and creative energy exchanges, except by this
mysterious attractive force in operation.

Why is it that each one of us will admit that "only
God can make a tree"? Is it not because we acknowledge
that we do not know how to make a tree? Molecules, in
response to some mysterious law of attraction, form in
never-ending patterns to give us trees, rocks, grass, an

---

[5] See *Science Is a Sacred Cow* by Anthony Standen (New York:
E. P. Dutton and Company, Inc., 1950), pp. 63-64.

infinite variety of blessings we refer to as "nature." Admitting only God can make a tree, are we not warranted in concluding that only God can make an automobile, a symphony, a pencil, a house, an infinite variety of things men live by? No single person on earth knows how to make an automobile, for instance.[6] Yet, there are 75 million of them in our country. How come? These things we enjoy and live by are not ours by reason of any single-minded human management. They are simply varied creative energies configurating, drawn together without any human's know-how, configurated by this mysterious law of attraction. Adam Smith observed this phenomenon and wrote that man, seeking only his own gain, is "led by an *invisible hand* to promote an end which was no part of his intention."

The Source of Man's Strength

Such metaphors as the Invisible Hand, this mysterious Attractive Force, Infinite Consciousness, and Divine Providence, are shorthand terms, so to speak, describing facets of man's experience with the workings of his Creator, God. Here we have Source, and it is man's highest purpose to seek it and to achieve as near a likeness to it as he can. This means to become as creative as possible, to grow in consciousness. Further, it means that

---

[6] Should anyone question the point that no person knows how to make an automobile, see my *I, Pencil* (The Foundation for Economic Education, Inc., Irvington-on-Hudson, N. Y.). Copy on request.

man should never, under any circumstances, individually or collectively, through government or any other agency, inhibit the flow of creative energies or creative energy exchanges. To hamper Creative Energy, in any manner, as it attempts to manifest itself in mankind, is to thwart Creation. Standing against Creation is no role for little, fallible man!

The above convictions must come under the heading of spiritual faith. It is only in this faith—only in this belief that man gets his rights, his strength, his consciousness from his Creator—that freedom among men is possible. For, individuals with this faith will never brook men or men-made authorities as the source of life, liberty, happiness, strength, consciousness. Faith in the Creator, if its implications be thoroughly understood, dispenses with all such nonsense. Society-wise, man frees himself with this spiritual faith. The intellectual and spiritual effort to achieve such a faith and such an understanding is the very lowest cost at which freedom comes. Any bids below this will never be heard, much less attended with success.

\

CHAPTER 2

CONSISTENCY REQUIRES
A PREMISE

IN THE PREVIOUS CHAPTER I argued that a faith in the Creator as the endower of men's rights is an appropriate foundation for libertarian leadership. I repeat, one admits this concept or he is faced with the alternative of submitting to the idea that men's rights are endowments of the state. There is no third alternative.[1]

Faith, however, is only the down payment, the cornerstone of the foundation for libertarian leadership. Subsequent installments concern the acquisition of a fundamental premise for oneself. This takes some difficult thinking—quite a price to pay! But freedom is not cheaply bought!

One of the great debates of our time concerns the role

---

[1] Admittedly, there are numerous distinguished economists—they call themselves utilitarians—who, by cause-and-effect reasoning, arrive at free market, private property, limited government conclusions. But the case for liberty should, in my opinion, be argued more along the lines of men's rights—justice—than along strictly materialistic lines. For more on this, see my *How To Reduce Taxes* (The Foundation for Economic Education, Inc., Irvington-on-Hudson, N. Y.). Copy on request.

of government in human affairs—government limited to defense of life and property versus government regulation and control of every aspect of our lives. Not that this is a new problem, for the proper role of government in society has engaged the attention of the ablest minds since the time of Plato. At present, however, the debate bogs down. The more the matter is discussed nowadays, the more confused become people's beliefs and the further they seem to move from any common understanding of the problem or agreement on the answer.

Our High State of Confusion

Never in all history has the discussion been on such a scale as now, never such airing of views—with practically everyone seemingly bent on setting all others straight. But the more that some people contend with each other over the issues, the more is discord promoted, the less is harmony achieved. Force, rather than personal freedom of choice and action, mounts the driver's seat. Why this unhappy state of affairs?

The reason may be nearer to home than most of us suspect. Few libertarian proponents of strictly limited government are sharply conscious of why they believe as they do. Nor have most authoritarians bothered to examine the why of their positions. Much less does either pretend to know or really care what is in the other's mind, or why. Obviously, persons with no fundamental premises of their own are unlikely to have anything fundamental in common with each other. So, let us first examine the *why* of our own beliefs.

The reason we do not know why we believe and act as we do is because we are not aware of our basic premise or prime value or fundamental point of reference. With our lives anchored to nothing, we tend to believe and act aimlessly; that is, we obey emotional compulsions instead of adhering strictly to the disciplines imposed by some transcendental premise or value or principle personally thought out and accepted. People swayed by a variety of emotional compulsions—acting outside the realm of reason and with no knowledge of what moves them or others—can find no common ground, regardless of how much they talk or fight. They lack a *common* premise; individually, they lack a *conscious* premise.

From Nowhere to Everywhere

Covetousness is an example of an emotional trait, as is fear of disapproval or desire for approbation. Suppose one person covets only political power and another only material wealth. With such diverse motivations, how could discussion lead them to agreement or even common understanding on, let us say, the TVA idea? The former would sense an advantage; the latter would think his ambitions thwarted. And the more logically they argue from such nonreasoned premises—from their emotional compulsions—the more widely would they diverge.

Marcus Aurelius remarked, "If you would discuss with

me, first define your terms." Good! But much more important and useful would be to say, "First, let us at least understand each other's premise, even though we may not agree." For it is fruitless to discuss economic, political, social, and moral subjects without first understanding our own premises as well as the premises of others. Otherwise, no party to the discussion can possibly know how to evaluate another's statements.

"What is your object in life? What is it you hope to achieve by your earthly existence? What, in your view, is your purpose here?" These would be appropriate questions to ask anyone who sees fit to argue about man's relationship to man.

Many people have never raised these questions with themselves, much less reflected on the answers. In this unthoughtful state, they do not qualify as instructors on questions of what's right and what's wrong in social, political, and economic affairs.

Man's Purpose

To arrive at a basic premise, one must ask and answer a fundamental human question: What is the goal of man's earthly striving; that is, what is life's highest value?

Is man's purpose here longevity, to extend creatural existence, stretch his life span?

Is it to accumulate wealth, pile up material possessions, get rich?

Should man aim to achieve supremacy over his fellow men, gain personal power, make others behave as he sees fit?

Ought man to expend his life's energies in trying to remake others in his own likeness; that is, become the ultimate arbiter of humanity?

Meaningless Motivations

With the questions put in this stark form, most people, even without prior reflection, would acknowledge that man is made for other things than these; he should have higher values. Yet, things such as these, in infinite variation, have served as motivations for countless actions, including those of "statecraft." Lust for power, glory, fame, title, notice, adulation, pomp, riches—all for a momentary show-off before earthlings—is about as much of a life goal as many people have. Try to discuss sensibly with people thus motivated a subject such as the scope of government!

Consider, briefly, the current rash of public discussions, debates, and "interviews"—radio, TV, and grand ballroom variety—and reflect on the why of their inanity. Of course, in the first place, they are designed mostly for entertainment. As the educational director (this was his title) of a national network said to seven of us prior to going on the air, "While we prefer that you not use profanity, don't let anything stand in the way of making this a hot scrap." Second, and by the very nature of these verbal brawls, the incentive is not to shed light but rather to out-clever one's adversary. And third—by far the most important reason for the puerile nature· of these insincere shows—is that no participant has the slightest notion what the other fellow's premises are, and may not know his own!

To demonstrate further the futility and the aimlessness of discussions where premises are in the dark, merely reflect on personal experiences with friends and associates. Note how often attempts to "talk it out" lead to nothing but sharpened awareness of disparity in viewpoints. Failure to understand each other's basic point of reference or prime value is more apt to yield bad feelings than harmonious conclusions.

What Is the Standard?

Consider again those two persons, one whose chief aim is political power and another whose major purpose in life is the accumulation of material wealth. They decide to discuss or debate the efficacy of the TVA idea. In all probability, neither is fully aware of his own motivation, and it is almost certain that neither is conscious of the other's basic point of reference. Should each argue logically from his own major object in life, the former would have to judge the TVA idea—government control and ownership of the means of production—to be consistent with his life's pattern; and the latter, seeking opportunity for private investment, would judge the idea to be inconsistent with his life's pattern. The longer they argue logically from their motivations—the further they move from agreement concerning TVA. It cannot be otherwise.

How much better if each were to start by examining his own premise and explaining it to the other! The first would confess, "I have no object or life value above that of political power." The second, "I have no object beyond that of great wealth." At this point they could conclude in unison, "It is useless for us to discuss the efficacy of the TVA idea. We should, instead, confine ourselves to a discussion of our varying premises. For, unless we can find a common or near-common premise, our reasoning and argument will only lead us astray and apart."

The variation in our respective life values is enormous. Some men want power; some riches; a few seek justice.

> Men have sought all sorts of other things—they have sought God, they have sought beauty, they have sought truth or they have sought glory, militarily or otherwise. They have sought adventure; they have even—so anthropologists tell us—sometimes believed that a large collection of dried human heads was the thing in all the world most worth having.[2]

Idle Nonsense

These comments are important and relevant. First, reflect on the senselessness of two individuals discussing

---

[2] See "Life, Liberty and the Pursuit of Welfare" by Joseph Wood Krutch in the Adventures of the Mind series, *Saturday Evening Post*, July 15, 1961.

social, political, economic, and moral matters, the life object of one being only dried human heads and the sole object of the other being riches. Arguing logically from such shallow premises, one would condone murder and the other would see nothing wrong in buying thousands of acres of land and having the government take money from other people to pay him for not growing wheat on it. There is no need to belabor the futility of such argument. *It is quite evident that all philosophical argument which does not proceed from a conscious premise is, perforce, a nonconscious argument—idle nonsense.*

Second, while there is no prospect of any substantial number of people thinking through and adopting a common premise, we can recognize a fairly general but vague search for such motivational background. Merely observe the attempt of people to "pigeonhole" others. Are they Republicans? Democrats? Socialists? Leftists? Rightists? Pinks? Reds? Physiocrats? Benthamites? Liberals? Reactionaries? New Dealers? Conservatives? Libertarians? These are fuzzy questions to which nothing better than fuzzy answers can be expected; nonetheless, they do demonstrate that many of us like to know what is at the root of people's actions and positions. If an individual's standard doesn't measure up to our own, we cross him off our list as unworthy of instructing us. Who would want advice from one bent only on collecting human heads? Or political plunder? Or coercive power over others?

Third, basic premises or life values are on a scale of their own. They range from bad to good, from hellish to heavenly, from evil to virtuous, from senseless to sound, from immoral to amoral to moral. In short, it does matter what one's major premise is—indeed, it may matter more than anything else in this earthly experience.

A "Good Will" Guide

A most admirable premise was developed and set forth by Immanuel Kant. His premise was that *good will* is the highest good, but he did not use the phrase as the equivalent of mere good intentions or general friendliness. The exercise of *good will*, according to Kant, is an affirmation of man's moral freedom by which he participates in the world of things as they really are, and acts in terms of his own nature. He wrote:

> Everything in nature works according to laws. Only a rational being has the capacity of acting according to the conception of laws, i.e., according to principles. This capacity is will. Since reason is required for the derivation of actions from laws, will is nothing else than practical reason.[3]

Kant's *good* was measured by whether he could answer yes to the question, "Can I will that my maxim become a universal law?" No rational being could will that lying or stealing or killing should be universally practiced;

---

[3] See *Foundations of the Metaphysics of Morals* by Immanuel Kant (New York: The Liberal Arts Press, 1959), p. 29.

therefore, lying, stealing, and killing must perforce be rejected as maxims for personal conduct. They are bad!

Kant argued that any discussion which makes no reference to fundamental principles (basic premise) produces a disgusting jumble of patched-up observations and half-reasoned principles. "Shallow-pates enjoy this, for it is very useful in everyday chit-chat."[4]

On the positive side Kant contended that a basic premise was indispensable "because morals themselves remain subject to all kinds of corruption so long as the guide and supreme norm for their correct estimation is lacking."[5] Each individual must, of course, determine his own basic premise or supreme norm, deriving as much instruction as possible from others who have seen fit to devise and accept basic premises for themselves.[6]

Certain Articles of Faith

While having only admiration for Kant's system of reasoning, my own adopted premise, though not inconsistent with his, is stated quite differently—certainly less profoundly—and is set forth for such reflection as anyone may wish to give it. My supreme norm or premise or

---

[4] *Ibid.*, p. 26.

[5] *Ibid.*, p. 6.

[6] C. E. M. Joad's *Decadence*, particularly the first eight chapters, is a brilliant explanation of what follows the "dropping of the object," that is, the disastrous results of not having high principles as premises. This book, published by Faber and Faber, Ltd., London (430 pp.), can be obtained from Humanities Press, Inc., 303 Fourth Avenue, New York 10, N. Y. $2.75.

fundamental point of reference has its origin in my answer to the question, "What is the purpose of man's earthly existence?"

Admittedly, the answer to this question has to be highly personal. It will vary according to one's fundamental assumptions. To me, it is self-evident that man did not create himself, for man knows almost nothing about himself. Man is the creature of God, or, if you prefer, of Infinite Principle or Consciousness or Intelligence. And there's more to life than the five senses reveal. Thus, these assumptions can be summarized as follows:

    a. A belief in the primacy or supremacy of an Infinite Consciousness;
    b. A conviction that the individual human consciousness is expansible; and
    c. A faith in the immortality of the human consciousness.

The Emerging Individual

For anyone with assumptions such as these, the answer to the question, "What is the purpose of man's earthly existence?" comes clear: It is for each individual to come as near as he can to the realization of those creative powers which are peculiarly and distinctively included in his own potentialities. *Man's purpose here is to grow, to emerge, to hatch, to evolve in consciousness, partaking as much as he can of Infinite Consciousness.*

If the above is accepted as the highest purpose of earthly life, it follows that any force—psychological or sociological—which binds or retards or in any way restrains the individual human spirit in its emergence must be thought of as an immoral and evil force. Conversely, the absence of such retarding and restraining forces—*the personal practice of freedom*—is moral, good, virtuous.

With this as a supreme norm or fundamental point of reference, it is easy enough to stand any and all proposals and propositions up against it and to form fairly accurate judgments as to whether they inhibit or promote a movement toward this ideal. Not only does this establish a basis for consistent action but it also permits others to judge whether one's moral, social, economic, and political positions are logical deductions from the acknowledged premise. Others may disagree with the premise, which is their privilege.[7] In this case the only discourse that makes sense must have to do with the varying premises. But, if the premise be adjudged satisfactory, then all issues can be intelligently discussed with enlightenment to the parties concerned.

Each an End in Himself

Be it noted that in the above premise, as well as in Kant's, each individual is assumed to be an end in himself. Anyone who acknowledges an Infinite Consciousness cannot help respecting fellow human beings as the

---

[7] "If a man does not keep pace with his companions, perhaps it is because he hears a different drummer. Let him step to the music which he hears, however measured or far away." Henry David Thoreau, *Walden*, Ch. XVlll.

apertures through whom Infinite Consciousness flows and manifests itself. Can man—any of us—predict which individuals will be most graced in this respect? Indeed not! Throughout recorded history the breakthroughs have occurred in the most unlikely individuals. Thus, it is the height of egotistical arrogance to doubt that each person—regardless of status, station, education, or whatever—is an end in himself. It would seem that no premise could qualify as good or moral *or libertarian* which fails to meet this qualification. Reason clearly dictates that "we treat humanity, whether in our own person or in that of another, always as an end and never as a means only."[8]

Reach for the Unattainable

In deciding on a supreme norm or fundamental premise for oneself it is advisable to select one that is unattainable; such, for instance, as the expansion of one's own consciousness—the more one advances, the more there is to be conscious of. It is a road of individual progress that has no end.

Consider this: A person has his eye set on scaling the world's highest mountain. This is his life's ambition, his only goal. Repeatedly he fails, but the challenge will not down. Finally, he succeeds and triumphantly stands in the rarefied air of his accomplishment—his mission achieved! No other object lies before him.

---

[8] *Foundations of the Metaphysics of Morals*, p. 47.

Reflect on the planning, the physical training—the growing in strength—that accrued to him so long as the object was before him. Now, contemplate what happens in the way of fading, weakness, atrophy, when life's deed is done, when there is no further object.

People arrive in a new land confronted with a wilderness. Clearing the forests and overcoming all the obstacles nature offers is their lot. Observe their development. Now, let them succeed, become affluent—their object realized, no other goal before them. Their moral fiber becomes soft, flabby; they become sloppy thinkers.

"Nothing fails like success," Dean Inge used to say; that is, no one can set himself an attainable object and, after its achievement, continue to grow. Thus, one's object ought to be of the unattainable variety, one that calls for perpetual striving, leading the individual on an endlessly emerging road.

Slavery Precluded

Reduced to the workaday world of practical affairs, a philosophy which concedes that each individual is an end in himself is a philosophy that precludes the practice of the few using the many as means. This philosophy is diametrically opposed to the socialistic scheme under which most of us unwillingly serve as means to the nefarious ends of those exercising unprincipled political power.

A high-principled premise for each rational human

being is seen to be of the utmost importance. Lacking it, there can be no sensible discussion of moral questions, and without such discussion there can be no foundation for a free society. The adoption and strict observation of high-principled premises will, on the other hand, result in as straight thinking and as consistently sound action as rational individuals are capable of. How well men and women do this determines the extent of freedom in society.

Yes, freedom depends on you. The individual is both its means and its end—the only foundation of freedom, and also its crowning object.

CHAPTER 3

BOOBY TRAPS

FEW IF ANY present-day workers for freedom have achieved effectiveness by relying solely on logical processes. This is to say that they did not begin by first developing a spiritual faith and then acquiring for themselves a fundamental premise or supreme norm. Such preparation has rarely been the means by which they got where they now are. Instead, they have become exasperated with the trends toward omnipotent statism and have plunged thoughtlessly into the fray, stumbling into one booby trap after another, and only if one of the lucky few, learning from their mistakes. It is not necessary, however, to take this costly course provided each aspirant will avoid the blind alleys experienced by those who have pioneered the trail.

When an otherwise preoccupied individual suddenly awakens to the authoritarian mess that increasingly engulfs us, his first impulse is to scream, "Let's have some action!" Then he begins to wonder what he means by action. Of course, he does not mean physical action, substituting his own physical force for the physical force he already detests. That would amount to no more than

47

swapping one brand of authoritarianism for another.
No, he doesn't mean that.

Educating the Masses

His impulse for action more often than not leads the
newcomer into frustrations. One wasteful booby trap
is the resolve to "sell the man in the street on free enterprise." Often it takes some such expression as, "We
gotta educate the masses."

Over and over again the argument is dinned into our
ears, "Let's stop talking to each other and reach out instead for the unconverted. Sell the masses on freedom;
they have the votes." This advice is superficially cogent,
with the result that hundreds of millions of dollars and
untold man-hours have been expended in an effort to
"bring light" to the masses.

But an impartial survey of these efforts fails to turn
up even one which lived up to its promises; all have
proved dismal failures. Nonetheless, the search for national salvation through "selling the masses" is as per-
sistent today as it ever was.[1]

If there is such a thing as "the masses," there must
be such a thing as a mass man. But who in heaven's

---

[1] Success in mass production anu sale of commodities—autos,
watches, soap, corn flakes, cosmetics—has influenced many to erroneously conclude that ideas can be mass sold. There is, however,
an important distinction between marketing products—things that
satisfy desires of the flesh—and spreading ideas, the latter being
accomplishments of the intellect. Commodities, once produced, are
ready for consumption, whereas "selling" an idea requires that each
"buyer" reproduce it in his own mind.

name is he, and where's his hangout? Perhaps he is among those who urge mass reform, for they are so numerous that the remaining population can hardly qualify as "the masses"!

Those who would "sell the masses" don't give us much of a clue as to the characteristics of the mass man except that he is low grade intellectually. He is always pointed to as one who needs vast improvement, so obviously he is something of an ignoramus.

Within these popular terms of reference, "the masses" who "don't understand" would seem to include the finger-pointers themselves. For, pray tell, who among us has a monopoly of understanding? Can it be those who insist that *someone else* be brought to a state of wisdom, especially when nearly everyone is pointing to someone else? Or, could it be that those who point their fingers are unwittingly pointing at their own reflections? Thinking they see someone else, they spend their money and time on the reformation of reflections and shadows, forgetting, as Thackeray put it, that "the world is a looking glass and gives back to every man the reflection of his own face." Small wonder that programs for educating the masses have so consistently met with dismal failure!

The "Mass Man" Defined

There is, though, a real mass man—millions of him! And he is not necessarily an ignorant fellow. By all the standards we use to measure intelligence, the best intellects among us may be of the mass. The real mass man is likely to be found in a position of leadership—in the church, in business, in the classroom, on the farm, and even more conspicuously in government and all committee-type organizations. This real mass man, I submit, has been escaping our attention because our natural inclination in the face of social problems is to seek the culprit among those whose behavior differs from our own. Using our own behaviors as the norm of right-eousness—"our" being the most of us—we find it difficult to discover the mass man in ourselves. It is almost unbelievable that *we* could be the masses.

How are we to recognize the real mass man—in others, or in ourselves? *The mass man is anyone who lives by a double standard of morality, who acts in the mass —the collective, the committee, the organization—in a manner inferior to the way he acts on his own responsibility.*

Joe Doakes Qualifies

Take Joe Doakes for example: he wouldn't kill a fly, let alone take the life of a human being. Yet, Mr. Doakes will join a mob, hang another by the neck till he's dead, and feel no remorse whatsoever. To his mind, the mob, not he, is responsible. Joe is definitely and definitively a mass man. For, Joe's moral standard when acting in mass is inferior to his moral standard when acting individually.

Most persons would agree that Joe Doakes fits the definition—but they themselves have never behaved like that! No, there aren't many lynching parties in this day and age. But, if the definition is accepted, the shoe will come nearer to fitting—and pinching—as we move on to more common examples of mass action.

For instance, suppose the federal government were to decree that all farmers are entitled to $30.00 for every acre of land taken out of production and that each farmer, with the help of an armed officer assigned to him for the purpose, is to call personally on people, rich and poor alike, and forcibly collect the booty. Disregarding the inefficiency of this cumbersome method, how many farmers would take advantage of such a law? Few indeed, for this personal, face-to-face procedure would be as revolting to the farmers as it would be to those from whom the pelf is taken.

Farmers in the Mass

However, let us give the immoral conduct sanctioned by this law the appearance of being depersonalized, rewriting it in conformity with the way it now stands on our statute books. Let the mass agency—government—do the forcible collection for the farmers. Nearly all feeling of guilt disappears. Indeed, in most instances, what would have been a feeling of moral revulsion gives way to an opposite sensation: *a right to the property of others*. This actually has happened to most of the million and more farmers now receiving such collections for not growing something. The action of farmers in the mass is inferior to the way each one of them would act personally.

Of course, it is not right to single out farmers as typical mass men. They qualify no more than do those of other occupations, such as the producer of steel products who wouldn't personally raise his hand to stop an exchange between two of his neighbors but who will solicit the help of the mass agency—government —to hinder and penalize certain exchanges in order to improve his own chance of getting that business. He has a moral standard for mass action inferior to his moral standard for personal action.

Depersonalizing the Act

Who in the church or the chamber of commerce would personally take the property of others by force to satisfy his charitable or welfare instincts? Except in rare headlines, such persons simply do not exist. Their personal standards of morality are above such action. Yet, the mere pretense of depersonalizing the act—doing it in mass, in the collective, in the organization— reduces their souls to the level of robbery. From the pulpit and in countless resolutions from every type of organization we hear and read solicitations to the federal pap-wagon, pleas for police grants-in-aids. These individuals—everyone who acts in this manner—are mass men, "the masses," whether their solicitations be for hospitals or airports or TVA's or subsidies for nonproduction or for anything else in the socialistic bag of tricks.

Apparently, it is the appearance of depersonalization that accounts for this destructive, inferior standard of morality. Joe Doakes thinks of the mob as doing the lynching, and so does each of the others. Everyone considers himself absolved of any evil, as if an abstraction —a mere term, "the mob"—could hang a man! But does action by a collective absolve the individuals who compose it of the responsibility for the collective action? An affirmative answer is absurd. The following story illustrates the point:

Saint Peter's List

A person reputed for his libertarian views was a visiting guest at a chamber of commerce meeting. Favorable action was taken on three committee reports, all of which were pleas for the federal government to use its compulsion to obtain the property of others that the local community might be "benefited." At the conclusion of the meeting the visitor was invited to "say a word." This is all he said:

> Remus Papwagon passed away and his spirit floated to the Pearly Gates. The spirit knocked. Saint Peter responded and inquired as to the purpose of the visit.
> "I crave admittance," said the spirit.
> Saint Peter looked over his list and sadly announced, "Sorry, Mr. Papwagon, I don't have your name."
> "Don't have my name? How come?"
> "You took money from others, from widows and orphans

as well as the rich, in order to satisfy your personal notions of doing good."

"Saint Peter, you are in error. I had the reputation of
an honest man."

"You may have had that reputation among those who
acted in a manner similar to yourself, but it was an
undeserved reputation. Specifically, you were a financial
supporter and a member of the board of directors of the
Opportunity Chamber of Commerce, and that organization sponsored a government golf course, to mention but
one of the many irresponsible actions that required the
coercive extortion of the earnings of widows and orphans
to benefit would-be golfers."

"Ah, but that was the Opportunity Chamber of Commerce that took those actions, not your humble servant,
Remus Papwagon."

Saint Peter looked over his list again and then said,
"Mr. Papwagon, we don't have any chambers of commerce
or labor unions or councils of churches on this list. There
is nothing but individual souls."

Saint Peter closed the Pearly Gates.

Whereupon, the meeting adjourned, but some in
attendance that day are still speculating on the where-
abouts of the soul of Remus Papwagon and on the pros-
pects for others who similarly deny self-responsibility.

Each of Us Is Guilty

A painful fact to keep in mind is that every living
person in the U.S.A. to some extent qualifies as a mass
man. Let each take note that any finger of shame points
in part at his own reflection. Absolute purity in conduct

in response to the dictates of individual conscience is
not attainable; it is only approachable.

If one would continue life—an aim this author com-
mends—there is no way to divorce oneself completely
from the way of life imposed by men who act in mass,
by men who act in some manner inferior to their highest personal standard of morality. Few, if any of us,
know how to live except in the market and in society
as it is. The very bread we eat is from subsidized wheat.
The mail that takes this book to the reader is rank with
special privilege, as socialistic as anything in the
U.S.S.R. Much of the power and light we use is on the
rob-Peter-to-pay-Paul basis. Our economic blood stream
—the money we use to exchange our millions of specializations—is shot through with the adulterations which
result from the Papwagon way of life. The only alternative to life in this smoggy atmosphere is death itself.

Absolute purity is unattainable. But we can paddle in
the direction of purity. So far as the mass agency—government—is concerned, we can refrain from ever standing sponsor for any socialistic activity, and we are free to
employ all the persuasion we can muster to explain the
fallacies of state ownership and control of any productive and creative activity.

Let Us Stand Personally Responsible

So far as voluntary mass agencies—committees and organizations—are concerned, we can, if we are a part of

them, act always in accurate response to our highest individual standard of morality, realizing that there is never any escape from a personal responsibility for any collective action in which the individual participates. And, one more thing: We can refuse to be a member or financial supporter of any voluntary organization that takes action for which we are unwilling to stand personally responsible.

Here is an example of how voluntary collectives all too often misrepresent us: A spokesman for a business organization appeared before a committee of Congress. By reason of what a small committee had resolved, he claimed to speak for several million businessmen. His report made concessions to rent control, concessions that many of the members would disapprove. In short, a lie was told. Many businessmen of libertarian views were represented as advocates of rent control, a socialistic item. Identity with such organizations is no way for a man to reflect accurately that which he believes to be right.

Nonetheless and more or less, we are all of the masses. And what we see as imperfections in others is little else but a reflection of how far we are from our own potential perfections. So, there may be something to "selling the masses" after all—that is, if each of us correctly identifies the individual seen in the looking glass as part of the mass and thus an imperfect man. Here is a fact so dimly appreciated it can be classified as secret: Further enlightenment of the man reflected in one's own mirror is the sole means he has of bringing more light to others.

"Put the Right Men in Office"

Then there is the booby trap of political action. It is not that there is anything wrong with politics per se, nor is this a suggestion that one should not take part in political activity. Far from it! *The booby trap is the notion that vanishing liberty can be restored merely by an increased or stepped-up political activity.* Ever so many people, when they finally wake up to what's going on, insist that there is only one kind of action: put the *right* men in public office.

The above summarizes a substantial, and perhaps even a growing sentiment. It stems from impatience. The interventionists, it is observed, have "leaders" galore in the political arena. Why, inquire many anti-interventionists, should we tarry any longer? Why not find ourselves some political leaders who will represent our points of view? Plans are then proposed for the organization of citizens down to the precinct level, and likely personalities are sought among renowned generals, businessmen, academicians, and others who have, in their own specialized fields, arrived at acknowledged leadership. It is assumed that the nation will be saved should they be elected to public office.

No Such Easy Solution

If this were the road out of the socialistic wilderness and if these miracle persons were to be found, all of us might consider joining the political actionist parade.

To take this route, however, is of no more avail than looking for the pot of gold at the end of the rainbow.

The reason that the interventionists have so many "leaders" is only because there is throughout our land a very substantial body of *influential*, interventionist opinion. The ones out front and who are popularly appraised as leaders are, in fact, not the real leaders. They are but echoes of the underlying opinion, and an echo implies an antecedent sound. They did not create the situation in which they find themselves; they are but the products or manifestations of the status quo. They, like actors in a play, merely move out front by reason of the fact that they can better articulate and dramatize the prevailing interventionist thought than can others. The real leaders of interventionism or any other movement, like playwrights, lie more under the surface, are a quieter breed, and not nearly as observable popularly.

First, the Foundation

Anti-interventionists lack "leaders" because there does not exist an influential libertarian opinion substantial enough to create the desired political response. What I wish to suggest here is the futility of attempting to build on a foundation that does not exist. One might as well look for an abundance of flowers where there has been a scarcity of seeds or listen for many echoes where there have been but few prior sounds. The out-front folks in political parties are but thermometers—indicators of the political temperature. Change the temperature and there will be a change in what's out front—*naturally and spontaneously.* The only purpose in keeping an eye on the thermometer is to know what the temperature is. If the underlying influential opinion—the temperature— is interventionist, we'll have interventionists in public office regardless of the party labels they may choose for their adornment and public appeal.

Influential Ideas on Liberty

If the underlying influential opinion—the tempera- ture—is libertarian, we'll have spokesmen for libertar- ianism in public office. Nor will all the king's horses and all the king's men be able to alter the reading of the political thermometer one whit.

It's the influential opinion that counts, and nothing else. This is to be distinguished from "public opinion," there being no such thing. Every significant movement in history—good or bad—has resulted from *influential* ideas held by comparatively few persons.

Here, then, is the key question: What constitutes an *influential* opinion? In the context of moral, social, eco- nomic, and political philosophy, influential opinion stems from or rests upon (1) depth of understanding, (2) strength of conviction, and (3) the power of attrac- tive exposition. These are the ingredients of self-perfec- tion as relating to a set of ideas. Persons who thus im- prove their understanding, dedication, and exposition are the leaders of men; the rest of us are followers, including the out-front political personalities.

To illustrate: How many persons today, or even in his own time of the early seventeenth century, ever heard of Hugo Grotius? Few, indeed, then or now! Yet, here is what the eminent historian, Andrew Dickson White, in the year 1910, wrote of this exceptionally important unknown:

> Into the very midst of all this welter of evil, at a point in time to all appearance hopeless, at a point in space apparently defenseless, in a nation of which every man, woman, and child was under sentence of death from its sovereign, was born a man who wrought as no other has ever done for a redemption of civilization from the main cause of all that misery; who thought out for Europe the precepts of right reason in international law; who made them heard; who gave a noble change to the course of human affairs; whose thoughts, reasonings, suggestions, and appeals produced an environment in which came an evolution of humanity that still continues.

One man altered the ways of the world. He achieved a degree of perfection that caused others to follow his insights and understanding. He spawned ideas that politicians emphasized and glamorized, and for which they more than Grotius became widely known as "leaders."

The Educational Way

In this day of our need how are we to find ourselves a Grotius, a Sarpi, a Turgot, or a thousand and one others who have quietly but brilliantly modified the

world into better ways? Those of us who would have any
part in working out this answer have no recourse except
to strive for an increasing perfection of ourselves, that is,
conscious personal efforts to become such helpful individuals. It isn't that you or I, specifically, will make the
grade. It is that out of a fairly wide creative effort in
which we participate some few will assuredly achieve
the competence our time so sorely requires. This is the
educational, not the political, way to mankind's improvement. True, it is slow in terms of one's life span, but it
has the distinct advantage of being the single practical
way there is. Let us try this way and witness its fruits!

"Time Is Running Out"

If we continue to exclaim—"I want action. Time is
running out"—and persist in the error of trying to reverse cause and effect, the political echo will continue to
confirm, "Time is running out."

Political leadership can only reflect influential opinion. There is no way to improve the quality of political
leadership except as we lift the level of influential opinion—and this is an educational task. "Tell me today
what the philosopher thinks, the university professor ex-
pounds, the schoolmaster teaches, the scholar publishes
in his treatises and textbooks, and I shall prophesy the
conduct of individuals, the ethics of businessmen, the
schemes of political leaders, the plans of economists, the
pleadings of lawyers, the decisions of judges, the legis-

lation of lawmakers, the treaties of diplomats, and the decisions of state a generation hence." The author of this wisdom is unknown, but history bears him out.

Superficial Anticommunism

A third blind alley is a narrowly conceived anticommunism. Contending against communism is to be applauded, but to regard the Moscow apparatus as the sole source of communism is to be led into a first-rate booby trap. Communism is a world-wide phenomenon and originates as much in the minds of Americans as in the minds of any other people. Were we to understand its fallacies and to reject its tenets, we would be impervious to the Kremlin's propaganda.

This booby trap was never laid better than by one high in our bureaucracy when he said, "The welfare state is the best security against communism."

This proposed defense against communism is not new, though we now hear it afresh. It has circulated in various shadings since "the cold war" began. A similar excuse was used to finance socialistic governments abroad with American earned income under the give-away programs that by now aggregate more than $78 billion: "Socialism is a good cushion against communism."

Such terms as communism, socialism, Fabianism, the welfare state, Nazism, fascism, state interventionism, egalitarianism, the planned economy, the New Deal, the Fair Deal, the New Republicanism, the New Frontier are simply different labels for much the same thing. To think that there is any vital distinction between these so-called ideologies is to miss the really important characteristic which all of these labels have in common.

An ideology is a doctrinal concept, a way of thinking, a set of beliefs. Examine the above-mentioned labels and it will be found that each is identified with a belief common to all the others: *Organized police force—government—should control the creative and productive actions of the people.* Every one of these labels—no exceptions—stands for a philosophy that is opposed to the free market, private property, limited government way of life. The latter holds that the law and its police force should be limited to restraint of violence from within and without the nation, to restraint and punishment of fraud, misrepresentation, predation—in short, to invoke a common justice. According to this way of life —the libertarian ideal—men are free to act creatively as they please.

They All Rest on Force

Under both the welfare state and communism, the responsibility for the welfare, security, and prosperity of the people is presumed to rest with the central government. Coercion is as much the tool of the welfare state as it is of communism. The programs and edicts of both are backed by the police force. All of us know this to be true under communism, but it is equally true under our own brand of welfare statism. Just try to avoid paying your "share" of a TVA deficit or of the farm subsidy program or of federal urban renewal or of social security or of the government's full employment program.

To appreciate the family likeness of the welfare state and communism, observe what happens to individual freedom of choice. Under either label (the ideology is the same) freedom of choice to individuals as to what they do with the fruits of their labor, how they employ themselves, what wages they receive, what and with whom they exchange their goods or services—such freedoms are forcibly stripped from individuals. The central government, it is claimed, will take over. Full responsibility for ourselves is denied in order to make us dependent on whatever political regime happens to be in control of the government apparatus. Do these labels mean fundamentally the same thing? As an exercise, try to find any meaningful distinction.

Words Without Meaning

Our planners are saying, "The welfare state is the best security against communism." The Russians could say, with as much sense, "Communism is the best security against the welfare state."

We call the Russian brand of governmental coercion "communism." They, however, refer to their collective as the "Union of Soviet *Socialist* Republics." The Russians call our brand of governmental coercion "capitalism." In the interest of accuracy and clarity, we, also, should call ours "socialist."

Socialism in Russia (communism, to our planners) and socialism in the U.S.A. (the welfare state, to our planners) have identical aims: the state ownership and control of the means of production. Further, one as much as the other rests on the use of police force. In Russia the force is more impetuously applied than here. There, they pull the trigger and think later, if at all. Here, the government relies more on the threat of force and acquiescence of the citizen.

Alexis de Tocqueville predicted over a century ago the characteristics of the despotism [the welfare state] which might arise in America: "The will of man is not shattered, but softened, bent, and guided; men are seldom forced by it to act, but they are constantly restrained from acting. Such a power does not destroy, but it prevents existence; it does not tyrannize, but it compresses, enervates, extinguishes, and stupefies a people, till each nation is reduced to nothing better than a flock of timid and industrious animals, of which the government is the shepherd."

There are countless other booby traps, some not so minor, like being drawn into TV, radio, and platform debates with the authoritarians, referred to in a previous chapter. These traps, however, will become apparent to anyone once he sets himself on the right course.

CHAPTER 4

WHY DO WE LOSE LIBERTY?

AT THE OUTSET, let me acknowledge that I do not know all the causes of authoritarianism. This is by way of saying that I do not know all of the reasons for governmental interventionism or why so many people are intent upon forcibly imposing their wills on others or why they attempt to cast others in their own little images. Further, I know of no thoughtful person who claims to know all the forces which make us behave as meanly toward each other as we do.

Yet, without some estimate of these causes it would be a waste of time, effort, and money to attempt a replacement of interventionism with freedom. Without a basic diagnosis of authoritarianism there would be no more chance of success in this venture than in trying to find the proverbial needle in the haystack, blindfolded. We cannot repair flaws without knowing where they are nor can we expect to correct error if we do not know *that* we err—and we will be aided in our corrective efforts if we know *why* we err. Therefore, any program aiming at free and willing exchange, at the practice of private property principles, and at limiting government to its proper scope, will require not only an awareness of existing deterrents to freedom, but also a reasonably sound hypothesis as to why they exist.

My object in this chapter will be to draw up an inventory of some of the errors, fallacies, failures, and blind spots which appear to give rise to authoritarianism. I will not attempt to discuss these in the order of their importance, for I do not know how they should be ranked —except for one blind spot that lies deeper than all the rest. At least, it is as deep in causation as I am able to probe.

Blind Spot: That Man Is the Creator

Persons unaware of a Creation, a Creative Force or Principle, an Infinite Intelligence or Consciousness, far over and beyond the human self are susceptible to a belief in their own omniscience. And those who believe in their own omniscience, logically, cannot envision a perfect society unless it be one in which others are cast in their fallible images. It is difficult for me to conceive of anything more responsible for authoritarianism than this type of unawareness.

If a people do not accept the Creator as Sovereign, as their Supreme Ruler, as their Source of Rights, they must, perforce, locate sovereignty in some mortal man or in some man-made institution. Logically, they must believe in and *accept* the one or *submit to* the other. If they locate sovereignty in government—a man-made institution—they have created an authoritarianism they must live with until they revoke it.

Failure: Inadequate Development of Self

All individuals are faced with the problem of whom to improve, themselves or others. Their aim, it seems to me, should be to effect their own unfolding, the upgrading of their own consciousness, in short, self-perfection. Those who don't even try or, when trying, find self-perfection too difficult, usually seek to expend their energy on others. Their energy has to find some target. Those who succeed in directing their energy inward—particularly if they be blessed with great energy, like Goethe, for instance—become moral leaders. Those who fail to direct their energy inward and let it manifest itself externally—particularly if they be of great energy, like Napoleon, for instance—become immoral leaders.[1] Those who refuse to rule themselves are usually bent on ruling others. Those who can rule themselves usually have no interest in ruling others.

Error: The Yearning for a Judas Goat[2]

Herbert Spencer called our attention to another type of human frailty from which authoritarianism springs:

[1] For an enlightening discussion of moral and immoral leadership, see *The Psychology of Leadership* by Dr. Franz E. Winkler (Garden City, N. Y.: The Myrin Institute, Inc., for Adult Education, 1957).
[2] Goats used in packing plants to lead sheep to their slaughter. They are trained to betray their kind.

Alike to the citizen and to the legislator, home-experiences daily supply proofs that the conduct of human beings baulks calculation. He has given up the thought of managing his wife and lets her manage him. Children on whom he has tried now reprimand, now punishment, now suasion, now reward, do not respond satisfactorily to any method; and no expostulation prevents their mother from treating them in ways he thinks mischievous. So, too, his dealings with his servants, whether by reasoning or by scolding, rarely succeed for long; the falling short of attention, or punctuality, or cleanliness, or sobriety, leads to constant changes. *Yet, difficult as he finds it to deal with humanity in detail, he is confident of his ability to deal with embodied humanity.* Citizens, not one-thousandth of whom he knows, not one-hundredth of whom he ever saw, and the great mass of whom belong to classes having habits and modes of thought of which he has but dim notions, he feels sure will act in ways he foresees, and fulfil ends he wishes. Is there not a marvellous incongruity between premises and conclusions?"[3] (Italics supplied)

Why is it that a person who obviously cannot manage himself, let alone those who are beholden to him, concludes that he is competent to direct a nation of people or the whole world when even the wisest of men would feel utterly incompetent for any such project. There appear to be at least two reasons. First, the inability to succeed in such "small things" as the management of self and of one's intimates leads to a frustration that can find no release except in affectations of grandeur. And, second, there are in any country countless thousands—often

---

[3] Herbert Spencer, *The Man Versus the State* (Caldwell, Idaho: The Caxton Printers, Ltd., 1944), p. 117.

millions—of psychopathic cases who are ready and eager
to follow such quackery. There are numberless people
who are always looking for a shepherd, and only an incompetent and frustrated person could ever aspire to such
a role. In short, there is a vast market for Judas goats.

Blind Spot: Inability To See Unheralded Accomplishments

The authoritarian who rises to the top, even though
a frustrated person as implied above, is always a person
of unusual energy, as suggested earlier. Being both ener-
getic and having the power to impose his will on others,
he gives the erroneous appearance of "getting things
done." He gives "bread and circuses" or "security" to the
masses, always at their expense, or displays a sputnik as
a great achievement even though it prevents millions of
daily, unheralded achievements by the people. This false
appearance of "getting things done" is accomplished by
depriving the people of freedom of choice as to their
activities and the fruits thereof and vesting control and
all freedom of choice in the dictator. Nonetheless, to
those who can see only highly publicized surface demon-
strations and who are blind to the countless accomplishments of free men, the dictator is attractive. Those who
wish to be told what to do and where to work and who
prefer to be hand-fed in exchange for their labors, become the dictator's supporters, and the more they demand of the dictator and depend on him, the less their
chance to know and enjoy the fruits of freedom.

Fallacy: Thoughts on Liberty Can Safely Be Left to Others

Our modern world is a highly specialized world. Indeed, we have gone so far into specialization that we tend to let others supply us with all of our needs except for our own specializations. This is unobjectionable if limited to goods and services. However, we carry the practice too far. There are some things we should not turn over to others. There are matters which require strictly personal attention. For instance, we should not turn our religion over to others, nor our integrity, nor our conscience. Nor should we be so foolish as to believe we can relieve ourselves of thinking seriously about liberty. Such thinking should not be delegated to any person, group, or organization. When all of us come to believe that the preservation of liberty is a responsibility that can be delegated, then liberty will have not a single defender. Authoritarians thrive in the absence of libertarian thinking like weeds in the absence of cultivation.

Error: If You Can't Lick 'Em, Join 'Em!

An increasing number of business leaders are concentrating on how they can accommodate themselves and their operations to the current governmental interventionism, not on how they can lessen the interventionism. Authoritarianism becomes very easy in any country where the business leaders cease their opposition to interventionism—as in Hitler's Germany or in Mussolini's Italy.

There is another aspect of this same distressing error: accepting membership on Boards of private organizations with collectivistic leanings, or positions in government bureaus having built-in socialistic designs, the intention being to "straighten them out" or, bluntly to interpret the motive, "to have them feel the impact of my *good* influences."

Getting in bed with the devil to reform him more often than not results in the reformer becoming devilish himself. This tactic has a sorry record; one needs but be observant to agree. The gospel of freedom cannot be effectively preached from within institutions headed in the socialistic direction. Outside their precincts, one is free to act on the dictates of his own conscience; but become a part of their machinery, and it follows that one must not only accommodate himself to, but put his stamp of approval on, the deviations and compromises implicit in such arrangements.

Failure: To Know Liberty in the Absence of Pain

There would be no tigers in zoos if they remained as ferocious as when first captured. However, they soon become docile, for tigers forget the freedom they once had and, forgetting, they have nothing against which to contrast their existing condition. Their confinement becomes their normalcy.

There never would have been any Negro slavery in the United States had the Negroes remained as intractable as when first taken from their African habitat. But, like the tigers, most of them soon lost consciousness of a freedom greater than the enslavement into which they were plunged. They became accustomed to their lot and, for the most part, accepted it.

The tiger and the Negro are in no way singular in this respect. We note on every hand this same easy and willing accommodation to the status quo, regardless of how onerous it may be. Americans who only a few years ago screamed like wounded apes at some intervention by government today may give that very same intervention their approval. Indeed, you can hear them exclaim, "How could we possibly do without it!"

It has been said that "the price of liberty is eternal vigilance." Yet, there are few persons who can be vigilant unless they are currently experiencing a restraint of a liberty they once took for granted. But, let the restraint persist for a short period and their aroused opposition will turn into compliance and finally into endorsement. Such persons merely add their weight to the interventionist movement. They aid authoritarianism.

Man, in the state of Grace or evolution or unfolding or emergence that characterizes most of us, is incapable of bettering himself except as he sees contrasts and faces and overcomes obstacles. All of nature seems to confirm this. For instance, we could not conceive of "up" if there were not a gravitational force pulling us down. Nor would there be any such word in our vocabulary as "light" if there were no darkness. The taking of a simple step presupposes something stepped on. Man, except as he achieves a higher state of consciousness than most of us can understand, cannot upgrade himself in an unobstructed universe. He requires what sometimes is referred to as "tension of the opposites" or "the law of polarity." The art of *becoming* rests on the practice of overcoming.

The late Paul Valery wisely observed, "The idea of liberty is not *primary* within us; it is never evoked without being provoked; that is to say, it is always a *response*. We never think we are free when nothing shows us we are not free. . . . The idea of liberty is a response to some sensation or hypothesis of impediment, hindrance, or resistance, which opposes itself either to some impulse in our being, or to some desire of the senses, or to a need, or else to the exercise of our considered will.

"I am only free when I feel free, but I only feel free when I think I am being constrained, when I start imagining some state which contrasts with my present state. Liberty is therefore not felt, nor conceived, nor desired, save by the *effect* of a *contrast*.

"This is the conclusion I must draw: Since the need for liberty and the idea of *liberty* are not produced in those who are not subject to hindrances and constraints, the less we are aware of restrictions, the less the term and reflex liberty will exist. A person who is scarcely aware . . . of the constraints which are imposed on him by public powers . . . will react hardly at all against these constraints. He will have no impulse of rebellion, no reflex, no revolt against the authority which imposes such restrictions upon him. On the contrary, as often as not he will find himself relieved of a vague responsibility."[4]

An intervention when first imposed causes change and, therefore, pain. But soon the changed way becomes the customary way, and no longer painful. "We never had it so good," chant millions of Americans as they become adjusted to an interventionism that already takes more than one-third of their earned income.[5]

Fallacy: Value Is Determined by the Labor Put into a Good or Service

The classical economists—Adam Smith, John Stuart Mill, and others—had no explanation of the market value of a good or service except the amount of labor that was used in producing it. It must be assumed that this explanation was not wholly satisfactory to such accomplished thinkers for it is so obviously wrong. Pursuing this theory, a mud pie would have the same value as a mince pie providing the same amount of labor went into the production of each. The classical economists, let it be said on their behalf, did not follow this labor theory of value to its logical conclusion for, had they done so, they would have come to the conclusion reached by Karl

[4] See Paul Valery, *Reflections on the World Today*, translated by Francis Scarfe (New York: Pantheon Books, Inc., 1948).

[5] See my "We Never Had It So Good," *The Freeman*, November 1960, p. 13 (The Foundation for Economic Education, Irvington-on-Hudson, N. Y.).

Marx: socialism. Following this theory, the makers of mud pies would have no way of being reimbursed for their efforts except as the government would take the fruits of the labor of others by force and subsidize the mud-pie makers.

Carl Menger of the University of Vienna, in the early 1870's, was, so far as I know, among the first to deny and displace the labor theory of value.[6] It was Menger and his followers who developed the free market theory of value.[7] This theory holds that the market value of a good or service is whatever someone will freely exchange for it. The free enterprise thesis is founded on this theory, just as the socialistic thesis is founded on the labor theory of value.

While, logically and intellectually, the labor theory of value is as outmoded as the-earth-is-flat idea, it none-theless persists to this day as a major cause of state inter-ventionism. Why, for instance, should we in the United States subsidize farmers and not subsidize bankrupt re-tailers except for the belief that farmers labor so much harder for their income than do others? Thoughtful analysis will reveal that it is the labor-theory-of-value type of thinking that lies at the root of labor union monopoly and coercion. The wage earner receives so little in return for his toil, goes the sympathetic think-

---

[6] Economists William Stanley Jevons (English) and Léon Walras (French) were independently developing the marginal utility theory of value at the same time as Menger (Austrian).

[7] This market method of price determination is often referred to as the subjective or marginal utility theory of value.

ing. The amount of effort expended, not what others will freely exchange for the result of the effort, becomes the basis for wage-earner compensation. No more with wage earners than with mud pies can an above-market price be obtained except by coercive force.

Authoritarianism on behalf of farmers and wage earners are but two of the ever so many instances of interventionism where the labor theory of value is the underlying cause. Any intelligent person can grasp its fallacy when explained in mud-pie, mince-pie terms. Few, however, appear able to retain in practice that which they conclude in reason.

Fallacy: A Wrong Can Be Righted with a Wrong

Examine the position of every person you know who classifies himself as a free enterpriser. In nearly every case the "free enterpriser" will endorse at least one item of interventionism.

A friend of mine in Belgium takes a free enterprise position when he opposes the U.S.A. tariff imposed on the blankets he makes. However, he is an exception maker, for he favors tariffs on the products coming into Belgium from the Belgian Congo on the grounds that the highly paid workers in Belgium cannot compete successfully with the lowly paid workers of the Belgian Congo. In short, the evil of low wages in the Belgian Congo must be compensated for by introducing a restriction to free exchange, a wrong to right a wrong.

Many American farmers justify support prices and subsidies on the ground that businessmen have their tariff.
They, instead of trying to remove the original wrong,
practice what might be termed "compensatory evil."

Cities and states apply political pressure for federal
aid to local projects. "Others are doing it," they claim.[8]
An eye for an eye; a tooth for a tooth! The whole economy is rife with efforts, not to remove economic plunder,
but to extend plunder.

Here we have the recipe for a concoction more poison-
ous than any witch ever brewed: Take the single exception allowed by each "free enterpriser." Put these countless exceptions into a pot. Stir vigorously, rapidly add-
ing emotion and self-interest unintelligently interpreted.
Bring to a rolling boil with a political apparatus. In the
name of accuracy and honesty list this dish on the menu
as "communism." Serve to every man, woman, and child
in the nation. Carry this message at the bottom of the
menu: "This dish has been prepared at your expense
by the free enterprisers of your country. You may not
like it but we find it is necessary for us to be realistic
and practical."

Blind Spot: Free Men Cannot Get Things Done

As the belief grows that coercion is the only practical
way to get things done—housing and medical care, for

---

[8] See my "We're paying for it, so we might as well get our share"
(The Foundation for Economic Education, Irvington-on-Hudson,
N. Y.). Single copy on request.

instance—the belief in man acting privately, freely, voluntarily, competitively, cooperatively, declines. As the former increases, the latter decreases.

In the U.S.A., for example, government has a monopoly of mail delivery. Ask citizens if government should do this, and most of them will reply in the affirmative. Why? Simply because government has pre-empted this activity for so many decades that all enterprisers have ceased to think how mail could be delivered were it a private enterprise opportunity. Indeed, most of them have come to believe that private enterprise would be wholly incapable of effective mail service. Yet, I note that each day we deliver more pounds of milk than mail. Further, milk is more perishable than a love letter, a catalogue, or an appeal for funds. We also note that the delivery of milk is more prompt and less costly to us than is the delivery of mail. I ask myself, then, why shouldn't private enterprise deliver mail? Private enterprise delivers freight. That's heavier.

But, no; my countrymen have lost faith in man's ability, acting freely, to deliver letters. Let us examine these people who have lost faith in free enterprise as relating to mail delivery.

Less than a hundred years ago the human voice could be delivered the distance that two champion hog callers could effectively communicate—about 44 yards. Free men have found out how to deliver the human voice around this earth—one million times as far—and in one-third the time.

Free men have found out how to deliver 115 persons from Los Angeles to Baltimore—2,600 miles—in 3 hours and 19 minutes.

Men, when left free to try, have found out how to deliver gas from a hole in Texas to my home in Irvington-on-Hudson, New York—1,300 miles—at low prices and without government subsidy.

Men, when left free to try, have discovered how to deliver an event, like a presidential inauguration, into every home, in motion and color, at the time it is going on.

Men, when left free to try, have learned how to deliver every 64 ounces of oil from the Persian Gulf to our eastern seaboard—more than half way around the earth—for less money than government will deliver a one-ounce letter across the street in my home town.

These men—miracle performers when free—have lost faith in free enterprise to deliver letters, and no longer question this activity as a proper governmental function. They consent to leaving mail delivery to government which employs the same methods in vogue a century ago and which presents the taxpayers with a $2 million daily deficit for the service!

Take a hypothetical example. Suppose at the beginning of our country's political establishment, some 185 years ago, it had been decreed that all children, from the time of birth to adulthood, were to receive "free" shoes and stockings from the federal government. Now, suppose this practice had been going on for all these years and I were to suggest that supplying shoes and stockings was not properly a government responsibility; that it was a family responsibility. What kind of a response would my suggestion evoke? Because free men lose faith in themselves when government takes over an activity, they would respond, "But you would let the poor boys and girls go unshod"—which our own experience shows to be an absurdity. I note that the poor children are better shod in countries where shoes and stockings are a family responsibility than where a government responsibility; that the poor children are better shod in countries where the people are more free than in countries where they are less free. A decline in faith in free men and what they can accomplish results in a rising faith in disastrous authoritarianism.

Blind Spot: An Inability To Explain the Free Society

I have never heard of a consistent socialist. That is, I am not aware of any person who believes that authoritarianism should be universally applied, that the state should forcibly direct and control *all* creative and productive activities. There are areas that the most ardent Marxist would leave to free will and volition. In short, there is hardly a person who does not balk at authoritarianism in some of its forms.

In the U.S.A. there are many millions of people who rant against communism, who inveigh against socialistic measures, and who raise their voices to high heaven at state interventionism, particularly if the intervention is directed at them. This negative force, however, does not constitute effective opposition to authoritarianism. Bad ideas are not removed by damning them.

Bad ideas, if they are to be rendered ineffective, must be replaced with good ideas. Herein lies a great weakness of the freedom supporters. Millions can damn authoritarianism but how few there are who can skillfully, persuasively, and attractively explain authoritarianism's opposite: the free market, private property, limited government philosophy! In the absence of this ability state interventionism thrives.

Fallacy: Authoritarianism Should Be Removed Gradually

Following World War II and prior to the relaxation of wartime wage and price controls, I made a speech entitled "I'd Push the Button." This title was taken from the first sentence, "If there were a button on this rostrum, the pressing of which would instantaneously release all wage and price controls, I'd put my finger on it and push."

This was regarded as a radical notion, radical in the sense of being so thoroughgoing that few persons shared it. However, if an act is morally wrong or economically unsound, the quicker it is abolished the better.

Many people seem to hold the view that the beneficiary of special privilege acquires a vested interest in his unique position and should not be deprived of it *of a sudden*. They give little thought to the many persons from whom the plunder has been taken. It makes no difference what example of wage or price control one takes—rent control is as good as any. Under this control people have been permitted to occupy someone else's property at less than the free market would allow. By reason of this fact renters have been privileged to buy more tobacco or vacations, or some other good or service than would otherwise be the case. The landlord has been deprived of the fruits of his own labor. Yet, when it comes to the matter of restoring justice, most people will think of the disadvantages suddenly falling upon the renters rather than the accrued damage done to the owner.

Imagine an habitual and successful thief. For years he has been robbing everybody in the community without their knowledge. He has a fine home, cars, servants, and is a pillar of society. Upon discovering his fraud, should his robbery be diminished gradually or should justice be restored to the community at once? The answer appears too obvious to deserve further comment.

People, when contemplating the removal of authoritarianism, seem to fear that a sudden restoration of justice would too severely disrupt the economy. The fear is groundless. During the early days of our New Deal we were the victims of the NIRA, the National Industrial Recovery Act, a system of wage floors, price ceilings, and production quotas. Originally, it was accepted with enthusiasm by most of the business community. Slowly, the fallacy of this nefarious program was realized. Thoughtful business leaders agreed it had to be repealed. But, many of them argued that the repeal would have to be gradual. To remove it at once would throw the economy into a tailspin. Then, one afternoon the Supreme Court ruled that NIRA was unconstitutional. As of that moment all of its regulations and controls ceased to exist. Did this shake our economy? There wasn't a noticeable quiver except that all indices of prosperity showed improvement.

The fallacy of the theory of gradualism can be illustrated thus: A big, burly ruffian has me on my back, holding me down. My friends, observing my sad plight, agree that the ruffian must be removed. But, believing in the theory of gradualism, they contend that the ruffian must be removed *gradually*. They fail to see that the only result of the ruffian's removal would be my going to work *suddenly!*

There is nothing to fear by any nation of people in the removal of restrictions to creative and productive effort except the release of creative and productive effort. And why should they fear that which they so ardently desire?

If, in reciting a few of the more or less obvious causes of authoritarianism, I have left the impression that the remedy is beyond anything that can be expected from ordinary citizens in ordinary effort, then I have made my point.

CHAPTER 5

EMERGENCE OF A LEADERSHIP

Every man, however obscure, however
removed from the general recognition,
is one of a group of men impressible
for good, and impressible for evil, and
it is in the nature of things that he
cannot really improve himself without
in some degree improving other men.

CHARLES DICKENS

A STUDY of significant political movements or vast social shifts will reveal that every one of them—good or bad—has been led by an infinitesimal minority. Never has one of these changes been accompanied by mass understanding, nor should such ever be expected. All movements have had their leaders. Always there has been someone "at the head of the class," always someone who knows more about it than others.

Using hindsight, we discover that the individuals who have been leaders came from strange and odd beginnings. No one of them could have been predicted ahead of time.

The leader of one movement, nearly two thousand years ago, was born in a manger. Recently, the leader of a bad movement was an obscure Austrian paper hanger.

From where will come the leader or leaders of our own required renaissance? I do not know; you do not know; the individual himself or herself does not know, for all of us are possessed of aptitudes and potentialities about which we are unaware. One point is clear: The leaders will be born of the renaissance itself. They will come from strange and odd places; from the poor as well as the rich, from the distaff side as well as the male, from those who have had little in the way of formal education as well as from Ph.D.'s, from laborers as well as captains of industry, from laymen as well as clergy, from only God knows where! We merely know that there will be a new crop of leaders.

Look Not to Politicians

In the kind of an open society here envisioned, we must not look for the type of leadership I have in mind from seekers after political office, that is, from those who vie for power. For, as Lord Acton warned, "Power tends to corrupt and absolute power corrupts absolutely."

Only now and then in history can we find a person who had power and who did not become drunk with it. Lorenzo the Magnificent inherited the headship of Florence. But he was not a ruler in the authoritarian sense. Like the chief executive officer of a well-managed company, he accorded everyone a wide latitude of choice;

he gave them their heads, so to speak. It appears that he limited himself to the inhibition of destructive actions. Not being corrupted by the power of his office, there was an outburst of creative energy and the Florentines led the Renaissance.

Another example can be noted in the person of Queen Victoria. She, also, inherited power, but used it sparingly. She gave Englishmen freedom in the sense that a prisoner on parole has freedom. She had the power to control them but this she relaxed and they roamed all over the earth building empire and, until then, an unheard of prosperity.

Leadership Must Come from the People

These examples, however, are historical accidents. They are exceptions to the rule. Certainly, in a society where public officials are democratically chosen, we find few instances of those elected deploring excessive powers, of any sincere attempts to limit themselves. The record shows the reverse to be true.

The ideal society, therefore, must severely limit its political officialdom, denying it any degree of *rulership* in the overriding sense. With this done, the leadership must spring from among the people. Unless there emerges in a society an aristocracy of high principle, that society can never be free.

With the above as a background, let us now examine libertarian leadership as it relates to the present political situation in the U.S.A.

From Left to Right

To grasp the freedom problem as we see it, visualize what a statistician would call a Normal Curve—fat at the middle and thin at the ends. Now, represent the population of the U.S.A. by vertical bands of this curve. Let the short band at the extreme left symbolize the few articulate, effective antagonists of freedom. Let the equally short band at the extreme right symbolize the few articulate, effective protagonists of individual liberty and its related legal, ethical, and spiritual institutions. Between these two bands exist the many millions, more or less indifferent, as uninterested in understanding the nature of society and its political institutions as are most people in understanding the composition of a symphony; who, at best, can only become "listeners" or followers of

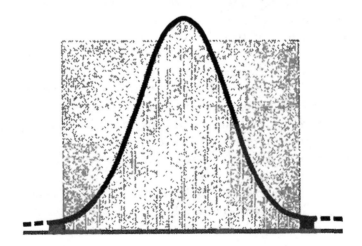

one camp or the other. A disproportionately large number of these are following the leftist camp today because those in the rightist camp are failing to do their homework. The ones symbolized by the band at the right are not manifesting the qualities of attraction and leadership of which they are capable. Thus, we conclude that the solution of problems relating to a free society depends upon the emergence of an informed leadership devoted to freedom.

In short, this is a leadership problem, not a mass reformation problem. If we had no way of remedying our situation except as the millions come to master the complexities of economic, social, political, and moral philosophy, we would not be warranted in spending a moment of our lives in this undertaking—it would be like expecting a majority of adult Americans to compose symphonies.

Libertarian Leaders Are Rare

If the problem is as we visualize it, then it is important to search for potential leaders with a devotion to those moral principles upon which the philosophy of freedom and, therefore, a free economy must rest. It is our conviction that, although these potential leaders are to be found in every walk of life, they may be as rare as composers of symphonies.

Assuredly, there was no large percentage of the American colonists capable of writing the Declaration of Independence, the Constitution, the Bill of Rights, or the Federalist Papers. Only a remarkable leadership from varying walks of life, small in number, understood the fundamental principles of a free society. And even a smaller number were able to write and speak about these principles. Fortunately, for the cause of freedom, there were such men as Jefferson, Madison, Jay, Samuel and John Adams, James Otis ("A law against Natural Law is void"), Tom Paine, and such business and professional stalwarts as Franklin (printer), Robert Morris (banker), John Marshall (lawyer), Benjamin Rush (physician), Charles Carroll (lawyer and businessman), George Mason (lawyer and farmer), James Bowdoin and John Hancock (merchants). Then, too, there were such "ordinary" citizens as Isaac Sears, John Lamb, Gershom Mott, William Wiley, Thomas Robinson. And reflect upon the leadership devoted to freedom among the clergy:

> JOHN WISE—The first colonist to justify village participation in local affairs by an appeal to political philosophy.
>
> CHARLES TURNER—"The Scriptures cannot be rightfully expounded without explaining in a manner friendly to freedom."
> "Religious liberty is so blended with civil, that if one falls, it is not to be expected that the other will continue."
>
> DANIEL SHUTE—"Life, liberty, and property are gifts of the Creator."
>
> RICHARD SALTER—"God never gives men up to be slaves until they lose their natural virtue and abandon themselves to slavery."

JONATHAN MAYHEW—"Their felicity is to be governed by such men and laws as themselves approve."

EZRA STILES—"Liberty, civil and religious, has sweet and attractive charms."

What our country requires is a reincarnation of the distinguished thinking and leadership that went into the making of America, able to frame the age-old dream of liberty in contemporary idiom. Nothing less will suffice.

Now, we must ask this question: How is this leadership to be developed? The answer is as simple to state as it is difficult to achieve. Let each one of us try to attain such heights in understanding and clarity of exposition that others—the few whoever they may be—will be attracted to do likewise by reason of the inspiration, however modest, we may be able to provide.

The solution of our problem rests on the emergence of several thousand (Who can know the number?) creative thinkers, writers, speakers—exemplars of a devotion to freedom. A realistic criterion for self-appraisal? Find an answer to the question, "Am I improving?"

The improving person will offer his findings—facts, evidence, ideas, arguments—to any and all segments of the population. If we show improvement, all those with an affinity for freedom who are within our range will be attracted to the improved offerings. This Law of Attraction is the only power anyone needs who would aid in showing others the way to higher levels of understanding. Upgrading of others is a *response to* the magnetism of superiority, the hallmark of an improving person.

CHAPTER 6

HUMILITY AND LEADERSHIP

*Three things prize above all: gentle-
ness, frugality, and humility. For the
gentle can be bold, the frugal can be
liberal, and the humble can become
leaders of men.*

LAO TZU

AN INDIVIDUAL does not adopt authoritarian ways because he knows so little. More likely than not, he be-
haves in this manner because he is unaware of how little
he knows—unaware of the significance that his personal
stock of knowledge has in the context of the whole.

But, first, what is meant by an authoritarian? Julius
Caesar, Napoleon, Mussolini, Hitler, Stalin, Perón qualify all right. The list, however, goes far beyond the few
who have gained renown as political tyrants. And it includes others in addition to Robin Hood, Jesse James,
Al Capone, racketeering labor and business leaders, and
the like who become governments on their own terms.
Further, the list includes more than the supporters of
political plunder—those who use the police force to take

from some and give to others; those who employ violence to support the claim that their ways of disposing of the fruits of your labor are better than your ways. The list must also include the intellectual authoritarians, those believing that all who do not see eye-to-eye with them are to that extent "off beam"—or fools. The authoritarians are a numerous lot!

Now, it is perfectly obvious that many authoritarians are richer in an encyclopedic type of knowledge than are many libertarians. But, does this necessarily mean that they are wiser? Socrates, reputedly wise, said, "This man thinks he knows something when he does not, whereas I, as I do not know anything, do not think I do either."

An Elusive Quality

It would seem that a person who has gained an awareness of how little he knows could hardly behave as an authoritarian. Such an awareness, however, must be exceedingly elusive; few seem to achieve it. Most of us assume that reality does not go beyond those things and events which fall within the purview of our five senses. We assume that other people are only what they seem to us; that the light we see is the light that is; that the sounds we hear and the odors we smell are the only sounds and odors; that we are the captains of our own souls and the lords of all we survey.

Persons unaware of a creation, a force, an intelligence, a consciousness, far over and beyond selves are susceptible to a belief in their own omniscience. And those who believe in their own omniscience logically cannot envision a perfect society except as others are cast in their little images. It is difficult to imagine anything more responsible for authoritarianism than this type of unawareness.

One young man, a naval chaplain, who is aware of how little he knows explained how this awareness took root in him. As a student at the University of Michigan, visiting the great library for the first time, he became overwhelmed with the fact that there were over two million volumes on its shelves! At that moment he knew that he didn't know much.

Expanding One's Horizons

One way to gain an appreciation of how little we know is by conscious effort to expose ourselves to ideas, things, experiences lying outside our own small orbits. For, if we aren't daily standing more and more in awe of everything within and without our beings, we can count on it, we simply aren't growing in wisdom. To illustrate how exposure to the wholly new can create an awareness of how little we know, visualize a sheet of black, infinite in its dimensions. Now, assume that in childhood one had carved out an amount of light—understanding—as symbolized by the small circle on the next page. But, in the years since, he has enlarged his understanding as symbolized by the larger circle. In the latter case, note the

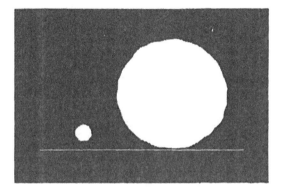

much greater amount of darkness to which he has ex-
posed himself. The more one knows, the more awareness
he should have of the unknown.

Inside the Atom

There are all sorts of helpful exercises—such as an
occasional rehearsal of the startling facts of life—that
can induce an awareness of how little one knows. For
example, while reading the above three paragraphs,
there will have been created within the reader nearly
one billion new red blood corpuscles. Astounding as this
is, each of these billion corpuscles is a mystery in itself.
For, "every substance is a system of molecules in motion
and every molecule is a system of oscillating atoms and
every atom is. . . ." Well, what is an atom?

One noted chemist in trying to make simple an answer
to this question began by asserting that there were more

atoms in his hand than there were grains of sand on all the beaches of the earth. To dramatize the nature of an atom he asked his listeners to take an Alice-in-Wonder-land growing pill, one that would shoot them through the roof, past the clouds, through the stratosphere, past the moon, past the sun and some of the planets, until each person was enlarged by a factor of a trillion. Thus magnified, an atom of calcium from the bone of one's thumb would be in manageable proportions for inspec-tion.

Electrons Circling a Nucleus

Enlarged by this factor of a trillion, the atom of cal-cium becomes a ball about one hundred yards in diam-eter. Inside there will be twenty luminous spheres about the size of basketballs moving in great circles like planets around the sun. These, says the scientist, are the elec-trons, the particles of negative electricity which make up the outer part of the atom. Some of them occasion-ally swing out and circle around neighboring atoms like folks doing a square dance, and this motion provides the forces which tie the atoms together in a chemical struc-ture.

If, continues the scientist, you try to find what the "sun" is, about which these planetary electrons are cir-cling, you have to look at the center of this calcium atom; and there you see a tiny whirling point of light, smaller than the head of a pin (after being multiplied 1,000,-000,000,000 times) . This is the atomic nucleus which contains practically all the mass of the atom, as well as its atomic energy.

If you ask the scientist what else is in the atom, his reply is, *"Nothing."* Since we are made of atoms, we, too, are nothing much but empty space. Apply an imaginary press to a human being and squeeze out all of the space, and there would remain a speck, smaller than a particle of dust that could be seen on a sheet of white paper!

A Greater Unknown

What is the lesson to be learned from such phenomena? Increase knowledge and understanding as much as one will, and the unknown, instead of being domesticated by man's mind, looms ever vaster and more improbable. We are not justified in believing that what we see with our eyes and what we hear with our ears constitute the whole of reality. Greater understanding is but a means to an awareness of the Infinite. No one of us gets more than a casual glance of all creation, and each of us experiences a different view.

Go a step further with our scientist. Consider the hydrogen nuclei in your own person. Now, assume that you know the secret of converting the energy of these nuclei into controlled electrical energy. You alone could supply power enough to operate all the factories and all the lights for the entire United States for many weeks. Or, suppose that you know how to fuse the hydrogen in your body. You could explode with a force one hundred

times greater than the atom bomb dropped on Hiro-
shima!

Just these smatterings of information leave me with a
feeling of utter awe, humility. I can now repeat with
meaning, "For I am fearfully and wonderfully made. Mar-
velous are Thy works." It is the next sentence, however,
that carries the greatest knowledge of all: *"And that my
soul knoweth right well."* Here is the soul cleansed of
know-it-allness, the precondition to fulfillment.

Thwarting the Creator

When the soul knows this about the self, it must, to
be logical, know this about others. It must know that in
each person there is an enormous potentiality, an un-
imaginable creativity, working to manifest itself, evolv-
ing, emerging. What human being, with any such awareness, could possibly suggest that his relatively ignorant
little will should be imposed on others, substituted for
this Creative Force? What person, thus humble, would
attempt forcibly to direct or control what another shall
invent, discover, create, where and at what he shall work,
what the hours of his labor shall be, what wage he shall
receive, what and with whom he shall exchange, or what
thoughts he shall entertain?

Assuming this awareness of how little one knows, how
could one behave as an authoritarian, play the role of
God? On the contrary, isn't it such an awareness that
can aid one in overcoming man's original sin, in thwart-

ing his continuous temptation, namely, the substitution of his will for that of his Creator?

Authoritarian attitudes and behaviors, however, are not to be done away with merely to relieve the pain of their affliction on others. Their destructive influence on the self which exercises them must be weighed.

Plato suggested that the real authoritarian is the real slave; that he is obliged to practice adulation, servility, and flattery. His desires are impossible of satisfaction and thus he is truly poor. He grows worse from having power; for power necessarily promotes jealousy, faithlessness, injustice, unfriendliness, and impiety. Not only is he miserable himself, but he also makes others equally as miserable. The authoritarian attempts to be the master of others when, obviously, he is not even master of himself. Plato likens the authoritarian to the man who passes his life, not in the building of his inner self, but in fighting and combating other men. Need we do more than look about us to confirm the rightness of Plato's observations?

Grow—or Die

Change is a law of all living things. That which is not growing is atrophying; that which is not progressing is retrogressing; that which is not emerging is regressing. *The authoritarian act, or even thought, is time off from growth, progress, emergence.* One cannot be attentive to the inner self while exerting coercion on others. The person who has me on my back holding me down is as permanently fastened on top of me as I am under him. To me, at least, this explains why Lord Acton was right when he said, "Power tends to corrupt and absolute power corrupts absolutely."

For any person to become aware of how little he knows —not a very difficult attainment—is a sure way to reduce the number of authoritarians by one. Who knows? The awareness might even catch on. And, if it did? Millions of us would forsake society's most corrosive pastime— meddling in the affairs of others—meddling not only through the political apparatus, but personally. Millions of us could then concentrate on the wholly rewarding venture of freeing ourselves from our own fears, our own superstitions, our own imperfections, our own ignorance. The individual human spirit, neglected while we play the futile and authoritarian game of imposing our wills on others, cries out for its freedom.

CHAPTER 7

INTEGRITY AND LEADERSHIP

SOME YEARS AGO the public relations officer of a large corporation summarized for me his guiding principle: "Find out what the people want and do more of it; find out what they don't want and do less of it."

While seldom so succinctly stated, such an external, "other directed" guide to behavior is finding ever wider acceptance in American life. Implicit in its acceptance is a flight from personal integrity; and here may be found an important explanation for some of the mischief presently besetting our society.

Doubtless, this is good enough as a formula for getting rich. However, if an individual looks upon wealth as a means to such higher ends as his own intellectual and spiritual emergence or realizing those creative potentialities inherent in his nature, then the formula has its shortcomings: in certain areas, it is downright destructive.

This is a serious charge. Let's explore it. In order to get this matter into perspective, contemplate the countless specialized subjects known to mankind. Take any

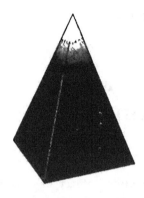

one of them—landscape painting, for instance—and arrange the population of the U.S.A. in a pyramid according to proficiency or quality. There would be some one person at the very peak. Under him would be a few competent l a n d s c a p e painters; there would follow perhaps one million having a discriminating appreciation of such art; after which there would be the great mass—millions upon millions, unconscious, unaware, utterly ignorant of the art or the standards by which its perfection could be attained or judged.

Rearrange the population in proficiency pyramids for all of the countless subjects which engage human interest and each of us would find himself near the base of most of the pyramids. Few are leaders or among the highly competent—except rarely and momentarily, if at all. Each of us has a potential for growth and development—especially if advantage is taken of the help available from those on higher levels.

With the above in mind, let us explore the implications of integrity to the situation we are contemplating. It involves the accurate reflection in word and deed of that which one's highest insight and conscience dictate as true and right. Now, a person's concept of what is true may not in fact be truth, but it is as close to truth

as he can get. It is the individual's nearest approximation to truth, his most faithful projection of that approximation, the most accurate reflection of his best lights.

Adverse Selectivity

With the pyramid picture and this conception of integrity in mind, let us now observe what happens when
the skilled in any subject—the competent who are near
the peak—adopt the practice of finding out what the
people want in order to "do more of it" and finding out
what they do not want in order to "do less of it." In
such circumstances, from whence comes the instruction
for what each of the skilled is to do? From the best that
is in each skilled person or available to him? From the
highest conscience of each? Indeed not! The instruction
and leadership in such circumstances is tailored to the
level of the "know-nothings" of the given subject, to the
values at the base of our imagined pyramid where over
90 per cent of the people are. Integrity is forsaken. Potential leadership is diverted from higher aspiration and,
instead, panders to the tastes and foibles of the ignorant
ones.

The fields of art and music, where new "lows" are
now so much in evidence, illustrate the flight from integrity. Consider the following confession, ascribed to
the famous painter, Picasso:

"In art, the mass of the people no longer seek conso-
lation and exaltation, but those who are refined, rich,

unoccupied, who are distillers of quintessences, seek what is new, strange, original, extravagant, scandalous. I myself, since cubism and even before, have satisfied these masters and critics, with all the changing oddities which passed through my head, and the less they understood me, the more they admired me. By amusing myself with all these games, with all these absurdities, with all these puzzles, rebuses, and arabesques, I became famous, and that very quickly. And fame for a painter means sales, gains, fortune, riches. And today, as you know, I am celebrated, I am rich. But when I am alone with myself, I have not the courage to think of myself as an artist in the great and ancient sense of the term. Giotto, Titian, Rembrandt, and Goya were great painters; I am only a *public entertainer* who has understood his times and has exhausted as best he could the imbecility, the vanity, the cupidity of his contemporaries. Mine is a bitter confession, more painful than it may appear, but it has the merit of being sincere."[1]

A Star Is Degraded

I have a TV program in mind. The star is an accomplished actress with an attractive voice. Does she sing the lovely songs of which she is capable?

Only now and then. For the most part, she and those in charge of her TV appearances insist on the stuff which

[1] Alan Houghton Broderick, *Mirage of Africa* (London: Hutchinson & Co., Ltd., 1953), p. 203.

nickels in juke boxes indicate as mass-popular. Instead of the millions at the lower part of the pyramid being lifted in their musical tastes by this singer at her creative best, we observe her descending and catering to the lowest or base tastes—an imitation of ignorance, so to speak. Thus is the music of our day degraded.

However unhappily we may view the wreckage which these responses to ignorance have brought to the fields of music, art, literature, entertainment, journalism, and the like, we must concede that the individual who cares anything about himself has the choice, in these fields, of turning off the TV and not reading or viewing the rubbish that is so overwhelmingly served up to him. He can, if he chooses, go his isolated, unmolested way.

In the Realm of Politics

But no such freedom of choice is allowed the individual when flight from integrity occurs in the realm of politics. The individual, irrespective of his scruples, his morals, his ideals, his tastes, is helplessly swept with millions of others into the miserable mess which the dull weight of ignorance gradually but inevitably inflicts on everyone.

A candidate for the Presidency, supposedly brighter and better educated than average, nevertheless polled the mass of voters to find what they wanted from government. As could have been foretold, they wanted the very things that crumbled the Roman Empire—"bread and circuses." The farmers wanted subsidies, not for outstanding performance, but for not farming. The labor unions wanted grants of coercive power that they might extort more pay for less work. Many businessmen wanted various protections against competition. Vast hordes wanted the guaranteed life: pensions, ease, retirement; in short, to be relieved of responsibility for self. These are the things our candidate professed to stand for and promised to deliver, if elected. Instead of standing consistently for the highest principles of political economy known to him, he imitated the lowest common denominator opinion of the population. His campaign manager confided that he had to do this to get elected; that once in office he would then do what he regarded as right. This opportunity never came; the candidate was defeated. And, defeat was his just due. One who runs a campaign without integrity proves openly that he would, at any time, forsake integrity if it appeared expedient for him to do so.

This explains why the two major political parties in the United States today stand for the same things. Both have chosen to receive their instructions from precisely the same source, the lowest common denominator of popular opinion. The result is a one-party system under two meaningless labels. This deplorable situation can never be remedied until there is a return to integrity, with candidates whose outer selves and actions will reflect their own best thoughts, regardless of the effect this may have on their political fortunes.

Edmund Burke, addressing those who had just elected him to Parliament, put the case for integrity in unequivocal and unmistakable terms:

> But his [the successful candidate's] unbiased opinion, his mature judgment, his enlightened conscience, he ought not to sacrifice to you, to any man, or to any set of men living. These he does not derive from your pleasure—no, nor from the law and the Constitution. They are a trust from Providence, for the abuse of which he is deeply answerable. Your representative owes you, not his industry only, but his judgment; and he betrays, instead of serving you, if he sacrifices it to your opinion.

George Washington had the same practical and lofty sentiments in mind when he reportedly said to the Constitutional Convention:

> If, to please the people, we offer what we ourselves disapprove, how can we afterwards defend our work? Let us raise a standard to which the wise and honest can repair. The event is in the hand of God.

Socialism Leaves Little Choice

No individual, whoever he may be, can escape the immediate consequences of ignorance in politics, as he can in art, music, journalism. There is no way to avoid the pains which bad political action inflicts. For ignorant political action encompasses all—one's life and the sustenance of life which is the fruit of one's own labor; one's freedom to choose how one shall live his own life. Political collectivism—the pattern consonant with political

ignorance—means what it says: Everyone swept indis-
criminately into a human mass, the collective.[2]

When an individual, in his thinking and actions, un-
hitches himself from integrity, he "lets himself go," so
to speak. He is anchored to nothing more stable than
whimsy, momentary impulses, mere whiffs of fickle opinion. He is adrift and without compass. This shows
through in much current art, music, poetry, and unquestionably accounts, in a very large measure, for the rapidly growing socialism, collectivism, decadence—call it
what you will. There remains, however, the task of discovering why integrity is so easily, casually, even eager-
ly abandoned. Why this wholesale divorce from personal conscience, this shameless acceptance of mass ignorance as our Director of Doing?

Error Compounded

Doubtless, there are numerous reasons, some of which
may be too obscure for ready discovery and examination.
One possible explanation has to do with a false economic assumption. We, having paid so much heed to
material progress and well-being, to ever higher stand-

---

[2] This dim view of political collectivism is not to be mistaken as
a backhanded endorsement of the "philosopher king" idea of Plato
and its modern counterpart: that society should be wholly governed by committees of the creative elite. There is no political
process of knowing or selecting in advance the persons who will be
most creative. The only process that will bring the creative minority
to the top, that will encourage their effectiveness, is complete
freedom.

ards of living, let our economic concepts pattern other aspects of our lives. Erring in our economic assumptions, we compound the error in our social, political, moral, and spiritual judgments.

Here is the error in economic diagnosis: We assume that "Find out what the people want and do more of it" has been the formula for our success, for our prolific production of goods and services. Thus, in the economic area, so we think, our guidance has come from the mass market rather than from conscience or higher realms of mind. The current cliché, "The consumer is king," tends to support this view.

The Spiritual Nature of Progress

Actually, instruction from the mass market has to do only with duplication. The market determines whether or not an economic good is to be duplicated and, if so, to what extent.

Duplication, sometimes called "mass production," admittedly controlled by the market, is not, however, the secret of productivity. The secret lies back of that. It has its genesis in the creation, the invention. Ralph Waldo Trine helps with this explanation:

> Everything is first worked out in the unseen before it is manifested in the seen, in the ideal before it is realized in the real, in the spiritual before it shows forth in the material. The realm of the unseen is the realm of cause. The realm of the seen is the realm of effect. The

nature of effect is always determined and conditioned by the nature of its cause.[3]

The noted economist, Professor Ludwig von Mises, reputedly the greatest free market theorist of our time, adds his judgment to this view:

> Production is a spiritual, intellectual, and ideological phenomenon. It is the method that man, directed by reason, employs for the best possible removal of uneasiness. What distinguishes our conditions from those of our ancestors who lived one thousand or twenty thousand years ago is not something material, but something spiritual. The material changes are the outcome of the spiritual changes.[4]

Where, for example, did Thomas Alva Edison get his ideas for the electric lamp? Not from the mass market! How could a people give specifications for something about which they were totally unaware?

In reality, the productive process works outward from that which is first presented uniquely to an individual mind as awareness or consciousness or insight (the reception of ideas—ideation) and is then accurately (with integrity) worked out or reflected in the material good or service. There is a distinctively spiritual accomplishment before the good or service is held up to view before the mass market.

---

[3] From *In Tune with the Infinite* (Indianapolis: The Bobbs-Merrill Co., 1897).

[4] From *Human Action* (New Haven: Yale University Press, 1949), p. 141.

Let Each Do His Best

American economic progress has been truly phenom-
enal. But this progress has been founded on inspiration
from the highest insights of individuals, not on advice
from the lower levels of ignorance. In this manner the
masses progressively are freed from poverty and slavery,
free men's material needs gratified as never before, and
opportunities opened to everyone to pursue and develop
those creative potentialities inherent in his own personality.[5] If we would succeed with our political institutions, we have in the productive process a model to emu-
late. However, we must understand how this process
really works: it finds its power in highest conscience and
the accurate reflection thereof, in short, in integrity.

One's highest conscience, regardless of the step it oc-
cupies on the Infinite Stairway of Righteousness and
Wisdom, is sensitive to the way one treats it. Lie about
it, distort it, reflect it inaccurately, take contrary instruction from inferior sources or yield to the temptation of
fame or fortune or popularity or other weaknesses of the
flesh *at its expense* and it will become flabby and flaccid
and will be incapable of rising to higher levels.

"To Thine Own Self Be True"

Now and then we observe individuals who can be de-
pended upon to state accurately that which they believe

---

[5] Touched upon here is the moral function of wealth. Whether or
not people use wealth to free themselves for higher effort is beyond
the scope of this essay. Many do not.

to be right, persons unmoved by fickle opinions, by the lure of applause, or by the sting of censure. We may disagree with such persons, but be it noted that we trust them. For their creed appears to be:

> This above all, to thine own self be true;
> And it must follow, as the night the day
> Thou canst not then be false to any man.

Such persons are possessed of integrity, an essential ingredient of libertarian leadership.

CHAPTER 8

THE METHODS OF
LEADERSHIP*

WHAT METHOD fits the objective of expanding freedom? This is the question to be considered.

At the outset, let it be conceded that the scope of freedom is without limit. There are, to begin with, the limitless psychological implications of freedom: man freeing himself from his own fears, superstitions, imperfections, ignorance. Then there is the sociological aspect: man freeing himself from bondage to other men—that is to say, from organizational and institutional ineptness such as governments gone berserk. Other aspects of this boundless subject: how to maximize individual freedom of choice, how to be free of violence, fraud, and predation in one's own nature and from others, and how to grasp the miraculous configurations of unique creative energies, once they are freed of restraint.

Freedom has to do with the "becoming" of the individual human being. All that retards the development

---

* This was published by The Myrin Institute, Inc., at Adelphi College, bearing the title, *Let the Method Fit the Objective.*

of the human potential is anti-freedom. All that advances the individual's wholeness or completeness as a spiritual, moral, and wise human being is freedom in action.

Now, then, how is the cause of freedom to be advanced? How can one person influence another to understand freedom? What means can be used to achieve such an end? There are good and sufficient reasons for this inquiry: Energies misspent and millions wasted on methods and techniques that do not fit the objective, account in no small measure for our rapid drift toward state absolutism.

Infinite and Variable Objectives

Man's objectives—good and bad—are endless in number and variety. Their attainment, in many instances, rests on how successfully he influences other people. But the method which is effective in attaining an objective at one level may be, and often is, entirely ineffective and inappropriate when applied to objectives of other levels. (A llama cannot carry a heavy load, but in the Andes he is the most efficient means of transportation.)

Said Emerson, "Cause and effect, means and ends, seed and fruit, cannot be severed; for the effect already blooms in the cause, the end pre-exists in the means, the fruit in the seed." This self-evident observation suggests that the accomplishment of any given objective waits upon a method precisely fitted to the objective. Here, then, is a hypothesis that merits serious examination:

The more destructive the end in view, the more fitting are compulsive means, disintegrative methods; the more creative the end in view, the more antagonistic to a solution are compulsive methods and the more must reliance be placed on attractive, integrative forces.

Methods Also Vary

Methods, like the objectives in view, range all the way from the low grade destructive types to the highest grade creative type. For example, almost anyone—the more ignorant the better—can effectively exert compulsive influence to achieve destructive ends: murder, theft, arson, defamation, and the like. The forcible collection of funds by government to pay writers to influence a whole nation to hate another nation requires less intensive compulsion than does homicide. Similar methods can seduce a vast population away from their voluntary, integrative, individualistic ways of life into collective or herd ways consonant with state absolutism.

Higher on the scale, there is an in-between area where the ends to be achieved may be either destructive or creative and in which compulsive and attractive methods intermingle: influencing others into a state of desire, often abnormal and obsessive, for drugs, alcohol, tobacco, cosmetics, soap, autos, houses, something-for-nothing, and so on.

At the upper end of the scale is education, or advancing other people's understanding. Such an aim falls into

the creative area. Compulsive methods, while often re-
sorted to, are wholly inappropriate and ineffective here.
Only techniques of attraction fit this objective. But even
here, we find that degrees and gradations exist. Creative
objectives, also, are on a series of levels, each level having
a technique peculiar to it: the higher the level, that is, the
more creative, the more must reliance be placed on the
power of attraction. For instance, advancing the understanding of another as to how to scramble eggs or master
the multiplication table or repair a motor or any other
skill where learning is acquired by mere repetition requires lower grade attractive power than does influencing others to paint beautiful pictures or write good
poetry.

The only reason for these brief observations is to rid
ourselves of that troublesome notion which leads many
people to conclude that the techniques used by communists, for instance, to destroy a free society can be
effectively employed to advance an understanding of
freedom. Or, further up the scale, that the techniques of
advertisers can be used effectively for this purpose.

A High Objective

Advancing an understanding of freedom is in a class
by itself. It is far higher in the scale of objectives than
those with which we daily deal, and the techniques required for its attainment are therefore of an unfamiliar
order. This order, it would seem, must be discovered

and applied if the status of freedom is to improve. Three decades of costly and dismal failures to advance an understanding of freedom have demonstrated that freedom will not be increased by methods beneath its majesty!

Who among us understands human freedom? Indeed, has anyone ever thoroughly understood its miraculous workings? I doubt it; I, at least, know of no individual, in the past or present, whose works are "the last word on freedom." The general, taken-for-granted understanding of freedom is little more than a false sense of know-it-allness that comes from knowing nothing at all. Understanding freedom, like gaining wisdom, may well belong to the realm of the sublime and the infinite.

Freedom is as high in the hierarchy of values as is the emergence of the individual human spirit and must be so evaluated by those who would advance an understanding of it.

One of the many reasons for the decline of freedom is that most of us erroneously accept it as an objective lower in the scale than it actually is and thus susceptible to the influence of techniques appropriate only to lower-scale objectives.

A Delicate Task

Once it is conceded that advancing an understanding of freedom belongs to as high a level as suggested above, we see that the problem is nothing less than influencing others to expand their consciousness, to increase their perceptions, to enlarge their cognitive powers. In brief, it becomes a question of the method one must use if he would influence another into a state of creative thinking. This problem transcends our common experience; it bears no relationship whatsoever to marketing or selling. Flashes of insight can no more be thrust into the consciousness of another or "sold" to him than he can be stabbed with a moonbeam! The simile may be apt.

A moonbeam kindles the imagination only as it is seen. It stimulates the mind only when perceived. Similarly with wisdom or the understanding of freedom. Wisdom is available for the perceiving. It appears to be in infinite supply, which is to say, regardless of how wise one may be, there is always more wisdom in store, more for the perceiving. Whether one is increasing wisdom or the understanding of freedom, the increase must rest on the expanding or stretching of consciousness—an achievement of the utmost delicacy and at the highest level!

In order to see how we may influence others in this respect, it is useful to examine how we ourselves are influenced. My own findings may be quite dissimilar to anyone else's but, as will be explained later, there is a sound reason for making one's own findings available to others.

Infinite Consciousness

To begin with, I have no way of accounting for such consciousness as man now possesses except to acknowledge the existence of an Infinite Consciousness. This force

—I confess to no precise knowledge of it beyond a personal awareness of its existence—appears to me to be an attractive force which persistently and everlastingly exerts a pull, a magnetic drawing of man into its infinite orbit. This is the force which explains man's emergence, his evolution. While there is never any relaxation of its drawing power, it encounters in each of us those human elements not susceptible to magnetism: arrogance, willfulness, know-it-allness. Emergence in the direction of Infinite Consciousness is thus in spite of, not because of, man's vaunted knowledge. This infinite force has many names in many tongues, among them God and Nature. Goethe, using the term, Nature, made a point relevant to this thesis:

> Nature understands no jesting; she is always true, always serious, always severe; she is always right, and the errors and faults are always those of man. The man incapable of appreciating her she despises and only to the apt, the pure, and the true, does she resign herself and reveal her secrets.

Freedom of Choice

Man, alone among animals, has arrived at that point in evolution where freedom of choice is a possibility. He is free, therefore, to respond harmoniously or disharmoniously to the attracting force of Infinite Consciousness. Since he is fallible his choices are often in error. Yet, viewed over the millenniums, the consciousness of many individual human beings is seen to have advanced qualitatively. Man has been spiritually attracted, figuratively pulled, upward and onward.[1]

Some individuals appear to be born less encrusted than the mill-run of us with obstacles to the magnetic pull of Infinite Consciousness. More susceptible to this force, they experience with relative ease such of its rewards as insights and inspiration. These persons are referred to as "intuitive" or "creative." With little effort they far surpass the rest of us. These few, over the centuries, have written our best poetry, painted our most beautiful pictures, composed our greatest music, done our significant inventing, discovered the important physical, chemical, mathematical principles, and so on. Time and again they have been asked, "Whence come these ideas of yours?" and they reply, in effect, "I don't know. It is as if they come out of the air."

Overcoming Inertia

For the vast majority of us the expanding of consciousness, the increasing of perception, the developing of intuitive powers, take a lot of doing. So much of our na-

[1] This power of attraction gives me the impression of occurring in waves—pulsating, as it were—and on countless frequencies. It is as if we were alternately drawn to or into its orbit and then left on our own. One frequency shows forth as a dark age, and the next as a renaissance. In daily life the individual experiences the rhythm of this force in shorter frequencies: as elation and depression, ambition and laziness, mental alertness and sluggishness, spiritual sensitiveness and insensitiveness, as if being led and as if alone, the perceptive apparatus turned on and then off, flashes of reason and return to habit—all in all, over the ages, man emerging from a Neanderthal state to produce occasionally a Socrates, Augustine, Goethe, Leonardo da Vinci, or Edison.

ture is immune to the attraction of Infinite Consciousness that we experience few of its rewards. We are as
sawdust to a magnet! There are, however, exercises and
disciplines that can aid Nature in her normal work, the
first requirement being a deep and profound desire on
the part of the individual for an expanding consciousness.

But, be it noted, this is an undertaking of the self-pro-
pulsive type. It is and can be set in motion only on one's
own initiative. No one on earth, by any technique whatsoever, can force another into this type of high-level
activity.

Infinite Consciousness is available *for the perceiving,*
either directly or indirectly. The former includes those
ideas, insights, inspiration which come to one "from out
of the blue." The term used to describe this experience
as it relates to Scripture is "revelation." This, so far as I
can discern, is not a common experience, but a person
can, with the right kind of conscientious effort, increase
enormously his own capacity to receive.

The Endless Pursuit of Truth

Now as to the indirect approaches: It seems self-evident that all the knowledge and wisdom available to
men on this earth today is a composite or aggregate of
insights so far revealed directly and accumulated over
the generations.[2] Certainly we cannot credit the present

---

[2] No question about it, much has been lost from this stockpile, for
man regresses as well as progresses.

emergent state of man to what we got from the Neander-
thalers. Over the ages the sum total of revealed truth is
beyond comprehension.

Infinite Consciousness is perceived by the individual
uniquely. No two persons among all who have lived
have intuited identically. No man has ever grasped more
than a portion of Infinity. At best each person has come
into possession of fragments, never the "Whole Truth."
The infinite aspect of Infinite Consciousness makes the
pursuit of truth or wisdom an endless undertaking.

So Many Sources

Thus it is that all the truth so far revealed to man
lies strewn over the earth in countless fragments—many
of them in books, perhaps in old books more than in the
new, often in languages few can read. Fragments of
truth are to be found among the living, a little in each,
not much in anyone. It is dispersed like a well-scrambled,
poly-billioned jigsaw puzzle. Find the pieces and put as
many together as possible. Look everywhere, overlook
nothing and no one. "Out of the mouths of babes. . . ."
The more success one has, the greater will be his awareness of the infinity of Consciousness; the greater the
knowing, the more will be the certainty of not knowing.

At this level there is no completion, no ultimate.
Nor need there be. The reward, the joy, is in the stretching—the stretching of the individual consciousness!

I have gone to some length to conjure up a mental picture of man when his objective is the search for truth, the gaining of wisdom. *Understanding freedom is of the same order and at the same high level!* First, there is The Source which the individual in the loneliness of his own soul can decide to heed and, to the extent of his ability, harmonize with. True, he can call on other individuals for guidance but it will be he and he alone who will make the decisions as to who those others shall be.

Others May Be Helpful

Second, there are all the mediating human beings, past and present, their utterances and their recorded works, not one containing more than fragments of the truth, *all unique.* Here we have the secondary source of guidance, and, as in the case of The Source, the seeker of truth decides himself which of the fragments he will add to his own stock.

Once we picture a person who is seeking enlightenment from The Source and from such fragments of truth as already exist in the minds and works of men, we can appreciate the futility of trying to "sell" freedom. *The selling or marketing method simply does not fit the freedom objective.* Conceding an Infinite Consciousness persistently exerting its attractive force on the obstinacy, arrogance, and apathy of man, and observing how slowly this greatest of all energies finds manifestation in human beings, what pomposity must we ascribe to those

among us who have no more than infinitesimal fragments
of this force, and yet would impose their "wisdom" on
others! They would surpass God! We are instinctively
repulsed by these reformers, and properly.[3]

The Reception Is Personal

No, the gaining of wisdom or the understanding of
freedom is not imposed by man upon men, nor can it be.
It is not marketed or sold. It is bought; but it is bought
only in the sense that an individual seeking truth will
look at whatever fragments he can bring within his purview and declare, as he alone sees fit, "I buy that!" This
is the process of personally perceiving that which is in
the realm of the available.

When an individual is drawn into the orbit of Infinite
Consciousness and perceives a portion of truth, that truth
can be said to exist in his consciousness; that is, he possesses a fragment of Infinite Consciousness. What he has
made his own is distinguished by its attracting quality
precisely as is its source; the latter differs from the former
only in the *force* of its attraction. The former is infinite,

---

[3] "For as He, who has all power, denies Himself any power over
us save that of love, to win us to love and obedience, so He would
have us use the same power whereby He has won us to Himself.
This is not sentimentality. On the contrary it is a hard saying. For,
because God out of love will never coerce man, will never use any
power but love to turn back to Himself; man is free to torture
and torment himself until he sees that his methods are not those
of his Maker." Gerald Heard, editor, *Prayers and Meditations* (New
York: Harper & Brothers), p. 39.

the latter infinitesimal. This is to say that truth is inherently attractive, regardless of where it exists."[4]

The Power of Attraction

The power of attraction is not outgoing but *ingathering*. It draws to itself whatever is susceptible to its force. This is at once its merit *and its limitation*. This is the given fact. In the context of the thesis of this book the power of attraction any individual exerts will bear a relationship to whatever of Infinite Consciousness he has been able to perceive, to whatever he has in store.

This idea is supported by daily observation. No person will knowingly seek light from one who has no light. Select any activity and ask: To whom are we drawn when seeking enlightenment? In golf, to a dub or to an Arnold Palmer? In cooking, to someone who never heard of a roux or to an Escoffier? In engineering, to one who knows nothing of stress or to an Admiral Moreell? In moral philosophy, to a bandit or to an Augustine?

St. Augustine is a case in point. Deeply contemplative and introspective, he experienced insights and understanding far surpassing those of most people. Bent on his own improvement, the expansion of his own conscious-

---

[4] This is not to argue that truth as held by man is *necessarily* an attractive force. Nor is truth the only attractive force. The power of attraction, as related to man, seems to bear some relationship to extraordinary skills. Great bull fighters or, vernacularly, great bull throwers draw people to them. Men who devoutly pursue truth, with a measure of success, and who achieve extraordinary skills in its exposition, give man-held truth its magnetism.

ness, he became a master of exposition; that is, he learned to explain the truth which came into his possession. In numerous writings, among them his *Confessions,* he made available to others that which he had first made his own. Today, more than fifteen centuries later, this is among the most widely purchased of all autobiographies! Here we observe the power of attraction extending itself remarkably in time.

Perfection of Self

Nor is the case of St. Augustine an exception to the rule. His case *is* the rule! It is this perfection of self which explains why we were attracted to Admiral Moreell—to use a contemporary example—to head the greatest engineering and construction project ever undertaken by man. Suppose that Moreell or St. Augustine, in the years of their relative immaturity, had called it quits, that is, had given up any pursuit of perfection, and had then gone about setting the world straight. St. Augustine wrote critically of his youth:

> But I wretched, most wretched, in the very beginning of my youth, had begged chastity of Thee; and said, "Give me chastity and continence, only not yet."

It is obvious that neither of these men would have developed any attractive powers whatsoever. Indeed, they would not have acquired those qualities which are susceptible to the attraction of Infinite Consciousness. They would have remained as human sawdust—unattractable and unattracting!

There is, however, one pitfall to be avoided. Most of us, when we move slightly ahead of our contemporaries, are prone to think of ourselves as "having arrived," as having graduated from immaturity. Thus we forego the further pursuit of truth in favor of badgering others with such fragments of truth as we have. There is no such thing as earthly completion; the term "maturity" is not in the grammar of The Infinite.

No Power of Compulsion

Man, be he St. Augustine or whosoever, can never know for certain whether his own insights—his little fragments—are in fact truth. We should be grateful, therefore, that truth can only attract but not compel. Imagine how destructive it would be to man's emergence, to the whole process of human evolution, if the tiny fragments any of us possesses could be thrust, forced, or impregnated into the minds of others! In brief, is it not encouraging, rather than distressing, that we cannot "sell" or "market" our own idea of truth as we can peddle material things? How reluctant we would be to allow anyone the power of forcing his ideas into our own consciousness! This would transform men into robots. Logically, we cannot accept as right for ourselves that which we construe to be wrong for everyone else, without ascribing a God-like character to ourselves. Heaven forbid!

In summary: Not only is it impossible to penetrate the consciousness of another with truth; it is un-desirable. Truth, wisdom, an understanding of freedom, an expanding consciousness are the highest of human aims and the methods of attaining them must be of an equally high order.

If freedom is to make any gains as a way of life, more individuals will need a better understanding of freedom than any of us now displays. This appears to be self-evident. Those who favor advancing an understanding of freedom are the only ones who can assist in such a venture. This, also, appears to be self-evident. But, how can they help? That's the question.

Life's Most Difficult Task

The method, not its application, is as simple as a-b-c. The solution lies in an expanding consciousness of freedom and its miraculous workings, and skillful exposition thereof by those who attain it. Consciousness—thinking, perceiving, understanding, attaining wisdom—is personal and individual. The only consciousness any individual can improve or expand is his own. Therefore, achieving the freedom objective involves nothing less than the widening of one's own consciousness! Nothing less than life's most difficult task.

Why is this simple solution so little recognized, as if it were a secret; or so hesitatingly accepted, as if it were something unpleasant? Why do so many regard as hope-less the broadening of the single consciousness over which the individual has some control while not even questioning their ability to stretch the consciousness of others over which they have no control at all?

Most of the answers to these questions are as complex as the psychoanalysis of a dictator or the explanation of why so many people dote on playing God. Leaving these aside, because I do not know the answers, there stands out one stubborn but untenable reason: *the widespread but desolating belief that the world or the nation or society could never be "saved" by the mere salvaging of private selves.* People say, "There isn't time for such a slow process," and then, to speed things up, they promptly hurry in the wrong direction! They concentrate on the improvement of others, which is a hopeless task, and neglect the improvement of themselves, which is possible. Thus, the world or the nation or society remains unimproved.

Said Victor Hugo, "More powerful than armies is an idea whose time has come." While incontestably true, this ray of hope presupposes the existence of ideas. We might as well admit it, there is a dearth of freedom ideas.

An Infinite Frontier

I find it helpful to think of Infinite Consciousness—wisdom, truth, the understanding of freedom—as an infinitely precious ore, buried deep in the human soul, the individual soul. This concept seems to square with experience, for no living person can mine any other ore than his own. But there is evidence aplenty that that spiritual ore is always available.

The object to be achieved is of the highest order: understanding freedom. The method must fit the problem. It can consist of nothing less than an increasing consciousness of freedom and the ideas appertaining thereto. Only an individual can mine this truth, this ore of awareness. This ore—Infinite Consciousness as it exists potentially in the human soul—is attractive but it cannot draw to itself disinterest, apathy, know-it-allness, these being no more than intellectual and spiritual sawdust. The first step to a "break through," as earlier suggested, is a profound desire on the part of the individual that such should come to pass. Only by seeking, striving, can the individual find and achieve; and the higher the aim the greater must be his effort. Nothing short of a will to a greater awareness can be susceptible to this power of attraction.

A Self-Mining Operation

In a sense the method that fits the freedom objective can be thought of as an intellectual and spiritual mining operation, each individual his own miner.

No individual, however, can extract more than a fragment of this ore of awareness. No one ever has and, assuming the finiteness of earthly man, no one ever will. The most productive miner—the most advanced creative thinker—who ever lived could not exist on the fragment mined by himself alone. He and his fellow men have existed—can exist—only by the pooling of their respective fragments, their intellectual and spiritual resources. We all exist by reason of the advantage we take of the *unique* resources of each. This appears to be another self-evident fact.

The method to fit the objective of achieving freedom takes shape, becomes apparent. It is, in short, for each of us to mine his own ore of Infinite Consciousness, re- fine it, and then make available, to all who seek, the distillate—the wisdom—unique in each fragment.

Enough To Do at Home

For this process to work it is necessary that one's eye be kept on his own mining, never on repairing the short- comings of others, never on inflicting one's own unique fragment on others. Indeed, it is important not only to refrain from any overt acts of this kind, but even from all covert thoughts as well. Intentions of reforming others, regardless of how skillfully disguised, are antago- nistic to one's own explorations. Further, they cause others, instinctively, to "run around the corner when they see you coming." But it is easy enough to cleanse the soul and mind of these intentions when once the attracting power of truth is appreciated. The seeker after truth should rely on it and should trust it to attract all that is susceptible to it, for Truth seems to shy away from those who lack faith in its power.

Explanations of what is discovered should be made in

speech and writing not as a means of repairing others but as the most effective way to increase personal exploratory powers, and—possibly—inspire others. Newly discovered ideas are but ore until refined with words, the tools of thought. Expositions devoid of any intention of making over others are attractive in proportion to the truth they contain. Properly, we give out ideas that we may further receive ideas. We teach: that is, we make available our discoveries, that we may learn more. Giving is a precondition to receiving.

So-called educational programs designed to repair the ignorant, when applied to the high-level freedom area, are less than useless. They only activate the existing ignorance, better left dormant.

Improvement Requires Humility

The method that fits an improved understanding of freedom begins with humility. The personal reasoning compatible with right method would seem to go something like this: To be honest about it, I know next to nothing about freedom myself. True, I favor freedom in a general sort of way but I cannot skillfully make the case for it nor do I know how to refute the clichés of state absolutism. I am woefully inarticulate. Attractive? Why, not even my wife or my children or my neighbors or my business friends or my employees seek my counsel. And, why should they? What have I to give? What is in me that they can draw on? Self-improvement assuredly is in order. Perhaps there are others in my circles of activities who would join with me in upgrading our individual selves. We could be of help to each other. My ideas, should I come upon any, might be useful to them; their ideas helpful to me. The more each of us improves, the more attractive will each of us become to the others. For one thing, I shall no longer attempt to insinuate my notions into the minds of others. Instead, I shall try to gain an understanding that they will desire to share.

Humility of the above brand never becomes inappropriate, regardless of how far one progresses. For progress in personal consciousness in the direction of Infinite Consciousness can never be more than a *relative* progress, that is, relative to where we ourselves were or where our contemporaries are. To realize one's potentials, it is only necessary to keep the eye cast toward an ever-increasing awareness or consciousness, taking no cognizance whatever of the minor superiorities over others one may achieve. People, quite naturally, are fascinated with, interested in, attracted to those who concentrate on seeking truth.

Reasoning suggests, and observations of the past seem to confirm, the attractiveness of truth. Its power is miraculous. There was one promise that should be borne in mind and unreservedly trusted: "And ye shall know the truth, and the truth shall make you free."

BIBLIOGRAPHY FOR CHAPTER 8

BENNETT, J. G. *The Crisis in Human Affairs*. New York: Hermitage House, 1951. (o.p.)

EDDINGTON, ARTHUR STANLEY. *Science and the Unseen World*. New York: MacMillan Company, 1929.

EULENBURG-WIENER, RENEE VON. *Fearfully and Wonderfully Made*. New York: MacMillan Company, 1938. (o.p.)

GHISELIN, BREWSTER (ed.). *The Creative Process*. New York: The New American Library, 1952.

HARDING, ROSAMOND, E. M. *The Anatomy of Inspiration*. Cambridge: W. Heffer & Son, Ltd., 1948. (o.p.)

HEARD, GERALD. *Training for the Life of the Spirit*. New York: Harper & Brothers, 1942.

HUTCHINSON, ELIOT DALE. *How To Think Creatively*. New York: Abingdon-Cokesbury Press, 1951.

JOAD, C. E. M. *Decadence*. London: Faber and Faber, Ltd., 1948.

JOHNSON, RAYNOR. *The Imprisoned Splendour*. New York: Harper & Brothers, 1953.

JUNG, C. G. *The Undiscovered Self*. New York: Little, Brown & Co., 1957.

NOUY, LECOMTE DU. *Human Destiny*. New York: Longmans, Green & Co., 1947.

WHITE, STEWART EDWARD. *The Unobstructed Universe*. New York: E. P. Dutton & Co., Inc., 1940.

WINKLER, FRANZ E. *Man: The Bridge Between Two Worlds*. New York: Harper & Brothers, 1960.

CHAPTER 9

THE MANNERS OF
LEADERSHIP

NEARLY ALL DEVOTEES of the freedom philosophy can re-
call acquaintanceships, initially agreeable, that went
sour.

"What a nice person!" we say when someone im-
presses us favorably. Be that person a housemaid or a
bank president, it is clear that neither education nor
occupation nor wealth have had any bearing on these
favorable associations. Graciousness, courtesy, amiabil-
ity, thoughtfulness, good will are among the virtues ex-
hibited by persons we have met from all walks of life.

All too often, however, the budding friendships come
a cropper. For, sooner or later, ideological inquiries are
made: How does the other stand on the role of government, human rights and property rights, profits, wages,
privileges, security, welfare, the right to a decent standard of living, the right to a job, or whatever? Then
sparks may fly and, unless caution and wisdom prevail,
an ugly trait, animosity, sets in.

Why does animosity set in? Isn't it because each

135

party, in the face of, sharp disagreement, tends to impute bad motives to the other? Selfish, power hungry, special pleader, fellow traveler, or reactionary are among the disparaging thoughts concerning the other; in short, the other is often regarded as either malevolent or a dupe.

The Mother of Animosity

Ascribing malevolence to another is the mother of animosity. It is the error at the root of social hatreds. And error it is! Among the persons known to me, I have never encountered anyone who appeared to be *consciously* malevolent. Not even a common thief is guided by malevolence. While he may not think of his occupation as the highest, everything considered, he believes it to be justifiable in terms of his scale of values. Indeed, it seems most probable that every action, by anyone, is thought of as right at the moment of action. Reflection afterward may bring regret but, on balance, most actions at the time of execution are assessed as right by the actors. Conscious malevolence rarely, if ever, controls actions.

If no person is consciously malevolent, then it follows that imputing bad motives to others is a mistake. And, if this be an alienating influence, then it behooves us who would make friends for freedom to discover what really causes the friction. Animosity need not accompany ideological differences if we know why the differences and if we correctly act on the knowledge.

The truth, sometimes, is difficult to acknowledge. If the following contention is in fact truth, it is a bitter pill to swallow: *The sparks fly because two varying degrees of ignorance clash head on!*

Now, ignorance is evident enough in the coercionists who would deny freedom. For example, no one of them—not even a dictator nor a ruthless labor leader—would put every item of human action under his control. Some degree of freedom would be allowed. But, no two coercionists agree as to just how much of human action should be coercively governed. If no two of them are alike, then it follows that not more than one of all their millions can possibly be right. Therefore, all except one unknown are plagued with some degree of ignorance.

Admitting One's Own Ignorance

The intellectual obstacle that has to be overcome is conceding a degree of ignorance in oneself. Though almost an unthinkable admission, in all good conscience, it must be made. While unable to prove it, I suspect it is my good fortune to be personally acquainted with more freedom devotees than any other person. Precise agreement among us? Indeed, not! No two see eye to eye. Not that this observed variance is to be condemned, but does it not suggest degrees of ignorance? Of course, it does.

Very well. Concede that it is the clash of two varying degrees of ignorance that causes these intense personal frictions, what then? Certainly, the most important step has been taken in making such a concession. Once this is done, the succeeding steps become more or less obvious:

A. Never get angry at the other person's ignorance. He has no monopoly on that. No doubt the other sincerely believes his position is right. The extent to which he cannot explain his belief is one measure of his ignorance.

B. Refrain from trying to force one's own ignorance on another. Self-ignorance can be measured as above—the extent to which a belief cannot be explained.

It is self-evident that the only way to overcome one's own ignorance is through *learning*. And, it is equally evident that teaching is the only way one can help to overcome another's ignorance. But a teacher is never self-designated; the teacher is selected by the person who chooses to be taught. Therefore, learning—teachableness —is the only way to qualify for teaching.

To Be Teachable

Let's further diagnose teachableness, for it is the failure to grasp this approach that is making enemies not only at the dinner table but at the "bargaining table."

For instance, a child insists that two and two make five. There is no reason to be angry at this, nor will anything be accomplished by merely asserting one's own

belief that two and two make four. If, however, one can
lead the child to *understand* that two and two do in fact
make four, the child will favorably regard his teacher
for such enlightenment. If, on the other hand, one cannot explain and shields his own ignorance, even if un-
consciously, by calling the child "dumb," "lazy," or "in-
dolent," the child will feel only hate for the inexpert
attention. All experience seems to testify that when ignorance clashes with ignorance the sparks will fly and
breed ill will, animosity. But when understanding and
clear exposition are administered to ignorance, affection
and esteem tend to flower.

So Few Can Explain

There are millions in America today who are taking
firm ideological positions, some on the side of governmental and labor union control and dictation, others on
the side of freedom to produce, to exchange, to live creatively as each chooses. But observe the small number on
either side who can do more than assert their position.
Only a few can explain with reason and clarity why they
believe as they do. This may be consistent behavior for
the coercionists, but there is no reason why those of us
who believe in freedom should follow their pattern. We
do not need to impugn the motives of those who have not
as yet grasped the significance of freedom nor do we
need vociferously to argue for points we cannot explain.
Quite to the contrary, we can turn conscientiously to our

own homework; we can aim at becoming competent ex-
positors.

There is an Arab proverb to the effect that he who
strikes the second blow starts the fight. Ignorance stands
ever ready, and all about us, to strike the first blow.
However, we need not strike back by projecting our own
ignorance—by insisting on points we cannot soundly explain. Short of an ability to explain our beliefs in an attractive, enlightening, and truth-serving manner, there
is always the friendly alternative of silence.

CHAPTER 10

AIDS TO LEADERSHIP

EVER SO MANY who write approvingly of FEE's education-al work conclude with the criticism, "But, you never tell us what to do."

Frankly, our editorial policy insists that we never tell a reader what to think or how to act. For, in our judg-ment, that is a certain way to alienate the very spirit of inquiry we hope to evoke. We have learned that ideas cannot be "crammed down the throat" of another. Ex-perience makes it plain that such attempts arouse only hostility. No one, however, resents taking a look at the ideas of another, regardless of the disagreement, provid-ing the ideas accurately reflect the author's genuine con-victions. This is why professors of socialistic persuasions sometimes write, "I don't agree at all with your position, but I admire the way you present your point of view and I read every word of it."

It is experience and reasoning of this kind which account for our presenting facts, evidence, ideas, and ar-guments *as we see them*. In our view, these are the in-gredients out of which convictions are formed. One's actions stem from one's convictions, but the form the action will take is peculiar to each person. One person will respond to a conviction in one way, another in a wholly different way. No two responses are exactly alike nor can anyone else make them alike nor is likeness necessarily desirable.

When people complain to us that we do not tell them what to do, they are really saying that we do not tell them how to act. Actually, this "failure" should be applauded, not lamented. Reflect on the nature of persuasive action, for that is the type of action in question. It is of two types: it is either physical or intellectual. Now, physical persuasion—coercion—as a means to broadening an understanding of freedom is patently absurd. Hence, nothing remains but intellectual action. Obviously, no one can compel a certain intellectual action in another. No one can do more than to suggest ways for inducing another's intellectual action—helping him find answers to a question that is intimately personal: "How can I go about improving the quality of my own intellectual action?"

Ten Thousand Leaders

Sticking to the context of advancing an understanding of freedom, the answer to that question might be found in the answers to another question, "What is it that the freedom philosophy most needs?" Clearly, the freedom philosophy needs most of all several thousand creative thinkers, writers, talkers—like Frederic Bastiat was to the freedom philosophy, or Poincare to mathematics, or Beethoven to music, or Milton to poetry, merely to give examples of the required quality. Needed are persons—shall we say 10,000?—from all walks of life who will serve as wellsprings of the philosophy. I, for one, do not see how any significant emergence of freedom is possible unless numerous high-grade *sources* of understanding and exposition come into existence.

Ten thousand Bastiats? Well, hardly. But it does seem possible for us to achieve that many reasonable approximations.[1] A big order, nonetheless. It calls for one such approximation from among each 8,500 of adult Americans. Who or where are the individuals with these highly creative potentialities? I repeat from an earlier chapter: I do not know. You do not know. The individual himself or herself does not know for the simple reason that all of us are possessed of creative potentialities about which we are unaware. Again, who are these unknowns? There is no answer except as each of us explores our own potentialities to see if "there's gold in them thar hills."

So Few Are Searching

There is gold aplenty, I am confident. The trouble is, to use a term in oil exploration, there just is not enough "wildcatting" going on. Too many of us are too lazy or

---

[1] Today, in the U.S.A., there are numerous persons who no doubt are superior to Bastiat as thinkers or writers or talkers, and their number is encouragingly on the increase.

too distracted by the trivia of life or "too busy." Others cannot see any point in trying out for a role where only one in thousands will make the grade. And even those who would try have given little if any thought to the techniques of exploring their own creative potentialities, to using what might be termed the "break-through" methods.

While there is a voluminous literature on unearthing creative qualities, it is not of the type that readily qualifies as "recommended readings." Instead, it is literature of the kind that strangely presents itself to a person's consciousness only if and when the individual is ready for it. And we can say that it does not really exist until then—in the sense that we can claim there is no sound of a falling tree unless there be an ear to hear it. It is like a verse in the Bible that one has known "by heart" since childhood and then, all of a sudden, had its profound meaning flash into consciousness. The words in the verse did not change; it was merely that one's perception changed, grew up, matured. Thus, with the literature on this subject. It does not exist for us until we grow to a point where comprehension is possible. Regardless of how much we grow, there appears to be no end to the supply that can edify. But, as I have suggested, this literature has to be self-discovered—as do one's own creative potentialities.

Furthermore, the literature helpful to one person will be different from that which proves helpful to another. Our vast variation accounts for this. In the common problems of life—how to repair a motor or master simple arithmetic or cook a beef stew—we can instruct each other, but as we move into the rarefied atmosphere of creativity, we get into strange and mystifying territory. Most highly creative or intuitive persons have found difficulty in explaining their own experiences and, therefore, have been at a loss to cite the reasons. Seemingly, their "flashes" have been wholly fortuitous. Poincare, one of the most brilliant mathematicians of our time, writing of the many ideas that came to his mind, said of one of his discoveries, "The idea came to me, without anything in my former thoughts seeming to have paved the way for it. . . . "[2]

And There It Was!

During the preparation of the first draft of this chapter, and at this very point, an associate of mine, with no awareness that I was writing on this subject, placed on my desk a magazine with the following paragraph marked for my attention:

> Everyone has his own frontier—in the mind. On one side of it, everything is known, tried. On the other side is the part of yourself that hasn't yet been explored. All life's great adventures are on that other side.[3]

Well, it is "that other side" which earmarks the creative area. The fact that we can do little to instruct each

---

[2] Henri Poincare, *The Creative Process* (New York: The New American Library of World Literature, Inc.), p. 37.
[3] John Kord Lagemann, "Meet the Champion," *Reader's Digest*, April 1959.

other in its exploration accounts, in no small measure, for the very few who ever make the attempt. Most of us prefer the beaten path; we do not aspire to stepping into territory never trod before, all alone.

There are, however, a few suggestions one can make that may aid in getting another started, tips on the shove-off—providing another wishes to take the plunge into his own unknown. Only a beginner, one taking his first steps, would have the temerity to offer counsel about an adventure so enormous. So, here goes!

The Mind Receives Ideas

The first step is the acceptance of a concept: *The conscious mind does not create the idea.* This mind is as a radio receiving set that can, if sensitively tuned, receive ideas. The recognition that there is a Creative Source outside of or over and beyond the conscious self cleanses the mind of know-it-allness and provides an openness, a humility, conducive to reception.

Next, as an essential precondition to the reception of ideas, to creative thinking, is a deep-seated, even prayerful desire that they be received. Ideas or insights appear not readily to come into consciousness except where they are ardently sought.

Fundamental, as in any activity, is practice or exercise. Biologists and physiologists know that the human brain has a seemingly endless supply of neuroblasts, the unfinished nerve cells, and that, potentially, these can, dur-

ing the span of life, be developed into neurons, the finished nerve cells:

> The potentialities of the human cortex are never fully
> realized. There is a surplus and, depending upon physical
> factors, education, environment and conscious effort,
> more or less of the initial store of neuroblasts will develop
> into mature, functioning neurons. The development of
> the more plastic and newer tissue of the brain depends to
> a large extent upon the conscious efforts made by the in-
> dividual. There is every reason to assume that develop-
> ment of cortical functions is promoted by mental activity
> and that continued mental activity is an important fac-
> tor in the retention of cortical plasticity into late life.
> . . . There also seem sufficient grounds for the assumption
> that habitual disuse of these highest centers results in
> atrophy or at least brings about a certain mental decline.[4]

Inducing ourselves to exercise mentally is more difficult than inducing ourselves to exercise physically. Knowing the need of physical exercise, I have never been able
to persist in a program of setting-up exercises. So I play
the pleasant trick on myself of indulging in golf and
curling.

Accept Each Challenge

Comparable opportunities exist for inducing mental
activity. Most individuals who have any competence in
the libertarian philosophy are invited to write or speak.
Do not be like the demure young thing who refuses
when asked to play the piano. Accept! Initially, this will

---

[4] Renee von Eulenburg-Wiener, *Fearfully and Wonderfully Made*
(New York: The Macmillan Company, 1938), p. 114.

require courage and many aches will ensue. It is like birth pains, for unused faculties are brought into play. But it is amazing how much thinking and study one will do—once an invitation is accepted—not merely to avoid making a fool of oneself but to appear to others as intelligent as he, in his secret heart, regards himself! The incentives in such circumstances are powerful, indeed!

Look for, rather than run away from, difficult questions posed by others. The search for answers seems to open spigots of the mind. Ideas hitherto undreamed of will begin to flow. The art of becoming is greatly improved by the act of overcoming.

A Chance To Learn

Let me now report the second instance, during the preparation of this chapter, which illustrates how oddly and coincidentally ideas come to one. Just as I was about to write this thought concerning mental exercise and ways of inducing it, a businessman of libertarian persuasions phoned. Said he, "Because of Jim Rogers' prodding, I have now accepted and delivered four speeches. And, am I learning a lot!" Here is the perfect example to illustrate my point. He is discovering talents that neither he nor his friends knew he had. Every speech of his will now become easier and better as will his reception of ideas. And, please reflect on the increased attractiveness and effectiveness of his informal conversations. He is becoming a source or wellspring.

Be patient. You cannot force yourself to have an idea any more than you can force an idea upon another. Feed yourself the problem to which you want answers, and then *relax and wait*. You must have faith that they will come. I cannot explain why this so frequently proves fruitful, but it does. It is quite obvious that the state of inspiration is not directly under the control of the will. No one can gain anything by saying, "Now I will be inspired." In fact, the only effort allowed by "the rules" is patient, regular work with the view of tuning the mind to a state of receptivity.[5]

Be alert. Ideas—call them inspiration, cognition, intuition, answers to questions, creative thoughts or whatever—have no conventional manner of presenting themselves. They come in countless ways, perhaps in a dream or as a thought-flash in the mind. Watch for the idea's appearance in the conversation of others; or, you may be reading a book and there it is! Quite often an idea will come in fragments, like a jigsaw puzzle, and the pieces may make their appearances weeks or even months apart. All of this may sound very mysterious, but it is no more so than a lily of the valley. We lose sight of the mystery in the commonplace while unfamiliarity accentuates the mystery in the uncommon.

Do not pin your expectations on some big idea and

---

[5] The last two sentences are paraphrased from *The Anatomy of Inspiration* by Dr. Rosamond E. M. Harding (Cambridge, England: W. Heffer & Son, Ltd.), p. 104.

by so doing miss the importance of its seemingly insignificant parts—the tiny idea. The grandiose idea, like the brain itself, is but the flowering of its little components. In short, count as success the discovery of a word or the shaping of a phrase that will improve understanding and communication.

An Open Mind

Formulate your ideas. Whenever coming into possession of an idea, work it out, think it through, develop its fullness, *at once*. Never permit an unformulated idea to clutter the mind. It must be hatched or, to change the metaphor, brought to bloom. Here is where conscious effort plays such an important role. For, unless an idea is gotten off the receiver and into memory, or otherwise recorded, the receiving set will not function with high fidelity. Indeed, one may get only "static." Two or three unhatched ideas make for mental confusion, the mind clogs or jams, and additional ideas, if they come, will be lost. The best way to do one's homework is to commit an idea to writing immediately on its reception.

Writing is the best way to formulate ideas, even to have ideas. One cannot formulate ideas in writing without thinking. Writing is a hard taskmaster, a severe discipline. It is easy to conclude that an idea is mastered —until the attempt is made to put it in writing. Instantly, many of its imperfections become apparent. An idea which cannot be written is an idea not mastered or possessed.

An idea once put to writing supplies improved words for speech, that is, writing adds to the fluency of speech.

There is an additional reason why writing should be adopted as a personal discipline. It has to do with another curious fact, the evanescence or flightiness or fading of ideas. All of us have had vivid dreams, yet the memory of them may be for only a few hours, sometimes for only a fraction of a second. Ideas behave in this same manner. So far as the memory is concerned, writing aids indelibility. However, it is the capturing of the idea for subsequent use or reference that counts. All of us have had thousands of ideas about which we are now totally unaware or, to quote Russell Dicks, "The infant mortality of newborn ideas is enormous."

Don't Let the Thought Perish

Parenthetically, there is another valuable point to keep in mind. It has to do with the premonitory or precognitive character of ideas as they flash into consciousness.

An insight or an idea as it impinges upon the consciousness—however ephemeral or evanescent the idea—*is a forewarning to the individual that he will be in need of it later on.* Unattended to, the insight will fade and one will not even be aware of having experienced it. Later, when the call comes for its use—in response to a question or when writing—there will be no more on hand than a vacuity. Attended to—immediately thought through and developed—the insight will exist as a personal, more or less matured reality, ready for use when its time comes.

Writers and conversationalists, respected for their range, depth, alertness, brilliance, are those who have taken advantage of that which has been offered them. They are the ones who have not postponed their homework but who have relegated to the past tense, as quickly as possible, the working out of all insights and ideas as received.

When the premonitory character of insights is more widely understood and believed than now, the infant mortality rate of newborn ideas will sharply decline.

A Daily Journal

May I commend the keeping of a daily journal in which ideas are formulated. Anyway, write the record of every day; for writing induces concentration and concentration is the most likely state in which ideas are received, in which they flow into consciousness. Let me quote Dr. Harding:

> The degree of concentration will clear the field of irrelevancies and enable [one] to tap ideas which under ordinary circumstances would be blotted out. If my theory is correct, the frequency of ideas *per minute,* so to speak, will be greatly increased under a powerful mood with its intense concentration. Under these conditions the mind . . . becomes, as it were, an intense magnetic field gath-

ering up ideas from realms of mind not possible under ordinary circumstances.[6]

To receive, it is necessary to give. Visualize a dam, back of which is a large body of water. From the dry side of the dam, insert a long pipe through the concrete so that it taps the water. Put a cap on the pipe. No water will flow from it; no water will flow into it. Now, remove the cap. Immediately, the potential energy of the lake becomes kinetic energy. Water will flow from the pipe; water will flow into it. This is energy in motion, energy at work.

A Flow of Ideas

Ideas are also a form of energy like the water. If you would receive ideas, then give off the ideas. Make them available to others. "It is more blessed to give than to receive" is a way of suggesting that giving is a precondition to receiving. Perhaps this is another way of saying that the best way to learn is to teach or, relating to our freedom problem, the best way to receive ideas is to speak and write about freedom principles. Liberty does, in fact, depend upon eloquence.

We should not overlook the time dimension. Most of us, when it comes to time, are not the captains of

[6] *Ibid.*, p. 135. "Magnetic field" may not be accurate. Perhaps it would be better to say that the mind, under intense concentration, becomes a powerful amplifier and thus can tune in "stations" otherwise inaudible. Also, it is apparent that intense concentration makes possible the tuning in of frequencies not possible under ordinary circumstances.

our own souls but instead are the victims of pressures, petty demands, trivia, weaknesses. One cannot concentrate and contemplate while viewing most TV programs, for instance. Nor can one receive ideas while letting the mind dwell on extraneous matters, or when one is angry, frustrated, depressed, or when one is scheming to remodel someone else.

Each person must discover for himself the mystery of time. Instead of being a circumscribing, confining, limiting element, time is in abundant supply. We make our own time, and thus time can be made elastic—responding, stretching, bending, expanding to accommodate our *higher* necessities. The reason why most persons complain that they "don't have time" is because they have no serious need for it. Be it noted that those who are creative and accomplish the most, strangely enough, are those who are, seemingly, the least pressed for time. Actually, there is more time for the really important matters than any of us ever knows how to use.

"Creative Quietism"

Now, here is an idea I have not succeeded in formulating to my own satisfaction. I am—how shall I say it? —intuitively certain of its importance but I have not yet discovered how to present it convincingly to many others. The idea has to do with a mode of behavior or method of working which Lao Tzu called "creative quietism." Reduced to practice, this means that we would not seek to make public figures of ourselves, but resolve instead to work with others in private seminars or in private study groups or in personal exchanges of ideas or in publishing material for private distribution. Aim to work privately as extensively as possible but shy away from becoming a public spectacle. Instead of seeking publicity, creative quietism suggests concentration on the perfecting of thought to which others will be drawn. Have no fear that one's light will be hidden; be confident, rather, that any light, if strong enough, will penetrate the darkness. Parenthetically, creative quietism is also the ideal way to proceed politically. If this method is used, those with libertarian beliefs will eventually occupy public office before the socialists know what has happened. For, nothing is so difficult to combat as that which is not known to exist. What I am arguing for might be dubbed "an underground on the top floor"— not secret but not showy; not impossible but not easy. Anyway, it is obvious that creative quietism is the way of working most conducive to creative thinking.[7]

No doubt the creativity manifests itself to some extent and on some occasions through everyone. Breathes there a man who never had an idea? Yet, the individuals

---

[7] "A new public opinion must be created privately and unobtrusively. The existing one is maintained by the press, by propaganda, by organization, and by financial and other influences which are at its disposal. The unnatural way of spreading ideas must be opposed by the natural one, which goes from man to man and relies solely on the truth of the thoughts and the hearer's receptiveness for new truth. . . ." Albert Schweitzer, *The Decay and the Restoration of Civilization.*

through whom this Creative Force abundantly and miraculously flows are rare, indeed. Only now and then does history show us such examples as Leonardo da Vinci, the man who was Shakespeare, Goethe, Edison. True, there have been thousands, but only thousands among the billions who have lived on this earth.

The general consensus has been that these geniuses were not only peculiarly endowed but that the rest of us are committed to a life of mediocrity. There are those, however, who take exception to this consensus about the rest of us, one of whom was an Austrian "mystic" by the name of Rudolph Steiner. He held that the creative potentiality was a normal human endowment, that this potentiality could to some degree be realized by many of us, providing we make the right kind of efforts.

Helpful Exercises

Steiner prescribed several exercises, but I shall present only the ones I have personally tried. These exercises cover a six-month period. If a day is missed in any month, begin the month all over again. These are designed to be habit forming, disciplines that have to do with one's thinking, feeling, willing; therefore, laxity cancels out any possible benefits.

First Month

> Concentrate for not less than five minutes each day on some object of your own choosing—a blade of grass, a leaf, a rock, a pencil, or whatever. Think of everything

you possibly can about this object—for instance, its source, even its molecular configuration, its purpose, and so on. But it should be *your* exploratory thinking, no one else's. One purpose of this exercise is to fix or identify you with reality, for any person who succeeds in a "breakthrough" is in danger of getting his "head in the clouds," whereas he should "keep his feet on the ground." The exercise stretches the consciousness remarkably. But, most important, is its development of clear thinking, controlled by self. It helps to free one from exterior influences like traditions, social positions, professions, nationalities, and so on—in short, to release one from being a mere reflex of one's environment. It teaches one to think about subjects of his own choosing without getting lost.

Second Month

This one, before it is tried, may sound silly. Its purpose is the development of personal will power. Most of us mistake our desire for approbation, our fear of opprobrium, and other motivations, for will power. We are prone to believe that we freely choose what we do more than the facts warrant. This exercise requires that you compel yourself to do something which has no utility whatever: Do something as useless as walking around a room once the first day, twice the second, and so on. The thirtieth day you will make thirty loops! Better do this one in the privacy of your own boudoir!

Third Month

Each day reflect on something which happens to you, be the happening good or bad. Bearing in mind that everything that happens to you has an instruction peculiarly its own, try to deduce what that instruction is. This exercise not only impressed on me how numerous the good happenings are relative to the bad ones but it sharpened my perception of important daily lessons that had been going unheeded. The teachings of the Creator, it seems, are not always in words, much less in English. Further, the exercise keeps one from being carried away with joy or depressed by sorrow or suffering. It helps to combat anger, irritation, fear, and to assure a personal equilibrium, a sense of inner quietness. Do not underrate the significance of inner quietness as a daily experience.

Fourth Month

For thirty consecutive days try to find the positive in the negative; that is, try to find something good in the bad. The good is always there. Example: Christ was warned not to cross a road because on the other side was something bad: the rotting carcass of a dog. Christ crossed the road and observed the good: "The dog has beautiful teeth."[8]

Fifth Month

Every day make it a point to reserve judgment. Refuse to draw a conclusion from gossip or hearsay. (Most newspapers and magazines will give you plenty of material.) Draw a conclusion only after you have personally come into possession of the facts.

Sixth Month

Repeat the five exercises, in their order, for six days each.

I must add that no one should even consider these exercises who is not temperamentally and spiritually ready and determined to become an improved person, *at whatever cost*. Such a venture should be entered upon happily

---

[8] This is from one of the Apocryphal Gospels.

but never lightly. To "toy" with these untapped and potentially powerful forces within one's own person is actually dangerous. Embark on this exploration conscientiously, or not at all. Further, this exploration, to be practically useful, must not be dissociated from one's workaday life. It is worth-while only if integrated with daily affairs, with such earthy matters as making a living.

It Is Easy To Be Destructive

In conclusion, I would have you reflect on how easy it is to make others angry or antagonistic or to take the fruits of their labor or even to kill them. These are popular forms of destructive influence. But, when it comes to creative influence—advancing the wisdom of another —we can do nothing, absolutely nothing, except as we generate in ourselves the power of attraction. This power, in turn, derives exclusively from depth of understanding and clarity of exposition or, shall we say, the measure of one's own wisdom.

In my judgment, a precondition to any realization of one's creative powers is the recognition of one's impotency. We must know how utterly powerless we are to cast others in our own images before there can be any emergence of our latent powers. For, be it remembered, we have not been given mankind to improve and reform, but only man—*one's manhood, if that can be found!* Does this appear like a project too minor? It is, in my view, life's one, great challenge presented at birth to each individual. No one can manage it except the individual and each will be graded on how competently he meets his own challenge.

I repeat, America's greatest need is for thousands of creative thinkers, writers, talkers—individuals who can, within their own circle of acquaintance and activity, serve as sources or wellsprings of the libertarian philosophy. No one can instruct another as to what he should do. No person can do more than attend to his own improvement and thus rise to the position where others will draw on him, call on him, invite him into counsel. This do-it-yourself project is one's only practical means of becoming valuable to others. And, have no fear about your own actions. You will act in response to whatever you become!

Unquestionably, it is possible for an individual, by the force of concentration and other disciplines, to tune in frequencies not usually perceived and thus gather ideas from many sources—from *The Source* and the emerging human sources where ideas are in supply. In so doing one will in turn become a source in his own right, extending his radiation as he progresses in his own fulfillment. This is the type of progress that might well be the prime aspiration of all who take the freedom philosophy seriously.

CHAPTER 11

THREE LEVELS OF LEADERSHIP

IN THE PRECEDING CHAPTERS, I have claimed that any widening of libertarian understanding rests on the emergence from numerous walks of life of a corps of creative thinkers, writers, talkers of the free market, private property, limited government philosophy with its moral and spiritual antecedents.

At the very least, this pronouncement has proved discouraging to many of those who accept its validity. Most people who are concerned about and opposed to the present interventionist drift have held out little hope that they, personally, could ever become creative thinkers, writers, talkers of this complex subject. Thus, many have abandoned any concerted effort: The goal seems too high for them to make a try.

While there is nothing to warrant any lowering of the goal, experience and observation now convince me that there are other ways in which one can be effective on behalf of freedom. It seems to me now that there is not just one but, rather, there are three distinct levels

161

of leadership potential. At least one of these is open to any individual for whom conscious effort is not an overpowering obstacle.

THE FIRST LEVEL—Achieve that degree of understanding which makes it impossible to join in or support, in any manner whatsoever, any socialistic proposal; in short, refrain from ideological wrongdoing.

To attain this initial level requires no "original" thinking, writing, or talking, but it is much more than an incidental step. It takes a lot of doing! For instance, to avoid supporting any socialism requires an intimate understanding of what socialism is, the misleading labels under which it appears, and the subtle ways it insinuates itself into social action and behavior. Few people are able to recognize the nature of a socialistic practice once it has been Americanized. They think of a policy as socialistic only as and if it is practiced by such avowed socialists as the Russians. To uphold freedom effectively, one must be able to identify and understand local socialism. Every American practice has to be brought under rigorous inspection and scrutiny and examined in the light of socialism's definition: *Government ownership and control of the means of production.*

I am not suggesting that it is possible or practical to divorce oneself completely from socialistic influences. Complete separation would demand no use of the mails, no eating of bread, no riding of planes or ships, doing without an economical supply of power and light in more than 1,800 of our cities, no selling of goods and services to socialistic institutions, and so on, ad infinitum. To live, one must accept the facts of this world, at least to a large extent.[1] But it is possible to so live as never to sponsor a single socialistic invasion into the social and economic structure.[2]

One further thought: Do not underestimate the enormous influences set in motion by a person who refuses to sanction or promote any wrong action. Pronounced exemplary qualities have unbelievable radiating powers. The individual who gives no offense to libertarian ideals—even if he be utterly silent—attracts emulators, sets high standards for others to follow.

THE SECOND LEVEL—Achieve that degree of understanding and exposition required to point out socialistic fallacies and certain principles of freedom to those who come within one's own personal orbit.

Obviously, it requires more doing to reach this sec-

---

[1] This is a delicate point and needs much reflection. For instance, how much government pap, in a "welfare" economy, should a person accept? This question is somewhat like how much sedation should a patient take? The answer to both questions is: as little as possible. Both pap and sedation are killers of persons as well as of immediate pain.

[2] The manager of a prominent business voiced the sentiments of many "leaders": "Yes, possible for you in your FEE Ivory Tower. But were I to take this straight and narrow path I would be so at odds with the socialistic demands of my community that I couldn't keep my job." This is mere speculation on the manager's part. He has taken his orders from his own guesstimates of the popular taste for so long that he fears to risk an instruction from his own conscience. Further, a job which can be kept only through wrongdoing is no more respectable than is harlotry.

ond level than to reach the first. This goes beyond the realm of abstinence and moves into the area of positive action. It demands that a person learn to articulate the understanding he acquires. Included are skills in talking and writing, the proper stance, and so on.

There appears to be no limit to how far one can go in improving oral and written presentations. These disciplines are always subject to betterment, regardless of how far one has advanced. To really know a subject is to be able to speak or write it as easily as replying "49" to the query, "What's 7 x 7?"[3]

It is at this second level of leadership that stance—one's attitude toward others—becomes of great importance. There is the inevitable temptation, once a person comes into possession of ideas new to him, to inflict the new "wisdom" on others, to reform them, to make them over in his own image. So far as the advancement of libertarian ideals is concerned, the effects of this tactic are the opposite of those intended. It will send scurrying not only foes but friends as well. Little more will be accomplished than to earn a reputation as "a pest."

If one will wait patiently for others to recognize his newly acquired competence—relax until others are ready to listen and share his views—closed minds will open and become receptive. Indeed, no person can gain access to the mind of another until the other lets him in. It is the other who has control of the doorways to his

---

[3] For an elaboration of this point see "Who Knows?" in *Notes from FEE*, May 1961.

own perception. Prior to his decision to let us in, we are helpless. The "eager beaver" shows bad stance, and is rarely if ever admitted.

Advancement of libertarian ideals requires that each of us understands that the higher grade the objective, the higher grade must the method be. For instance, if one's objective were to destroy another, low-grade methods would suffice. But if the objective be the expansion of another's consciousness or the increasing of his wisdom, then only high-grade methods can be effective. Advancing an understanding of libertarian ideals belongs to the same hierarchy of values as does the expansion of consciousness and the increasing of wisdom.[4] In this respect, we can do nothing *to* others; we can only do something *for* them, and then only if we have something in store to give. We must recognize our limitations before we can begin to realize our potentialities.

THE THIRD LEVEL—Achieve that degree of excellence in understanding and exposition which will inspire others to seek one out as a tutor of the libertarian philosophy.

This is the level attained by the *creative* thinker, writer, talker, the level at which the power of attraction comes into play.

All of us are aware of creative persons in various fields: religion, music, poetry, art, mathematics, the physical

---

[4] See Chapter 8.

sciences, engineering, indeed, in all of the disciplines. These persons, as a rule, have reached their high status through practice, and concentration on self-perfection. A person becomes so rich in understanding and so inventive in explaining what he has learned or perceived that others, having ambitions for higher understanding, are drawn to him, that is, they *seek him out* as a tutor.

An individual may be sought as a tutor by only one or by millions; for a short period or for centuries. St. Augustine's *Confessions,* today, is among the most widely purchased of all autobiographies. That man, fifteen centuries after his passing, is still sought as a tutor by untold numbers, a measure of immortality, so to speak.

Reflect on the eminent naturalist, Luther Burbank. His work in his chosen field may have been as creative as man ever achieves. By turning his sights inward, that is, toward his own perfection, he experienced ideas, insights, inspiration, inventiveness. The garden spots of the world are richer and more beautiful by reason of this man's creative conduct. Suppose he had decided to concentrate, instead, on the shortcomings of others by calling attention to their unkempt gardens! He would have been remembered only as a muckraker and the earth would have been left less, not more, beautiful by reason of his existence. No one would have sought him as a tutor.

The creative thinker, writer, talker of libertarian ideals concentrates on the perfecting of his own understanding and on discovering effective ways to communicate such light as he possesses. Effort, of the deeply conscious variety, may result in a new parable, an enlightening analogy or homology, minor literary inventions that cause another to remark: "Now I see what you mean."

For instance, it has long been our contention that: "The fiscal concomitant of state welfarism or intervention is inflation. Politically, it is impossible to finance socialism by any other means. Therefore, for those of us who do not like inflation, only one recourse is open —*divest government of its power to practice socialism.*"[5] Such a statement is formal and difficult to grasp, thus, it needs some sort of an analogy to dramatize the point, such as:

> A good economy, in one respect, resembles a sponge. A sponge can sop up a lot of mess but when it becomes saturated the sponge itself is a mess. For the sponge to be useful again, the mess has to be wrung out of it.

Examples of creative thinkers who are sought as tutors? Adam Smith performed in this respect so well that he, more than any other, was responsible for the Industrial Revolution. Carl Menger discovered the marginal utility theory of value on which the free market rests; Eugen Böhm-Bawerk invented ways to explain the theory. His student, Ludwig von Mises, among his many findings,

---

[5] For an explanation from which this conclusion is drawn, see *Liberty: A Path to Its Recovery* by F. A. Harper, pp. 106-113 (The Foundation for Economic Education, Inc., Irvington-on-Hudson, N. Y. Cloth $2.00; paper $1.50).

discovered that there is no valid basis for making market judgments in a state of socialism. And think of the Hayeks, Hazlitts, Fertigs, and countless others who have sought the tutorship of Mises. Many of these students, in turn, have been sought as tutors. Among our contemporaries, I can now name several hundred who qualify as creative thinkers, writers, talkers of the libertarian philosophy whom others seek out as tutors. But to name them would do offense to the hundreds about whom I have never heard.

Yes, there are at least these three possible levels of libertarian leadership. Plainly, no one can start at the third level, or at the second. The first level must be attained first, and the second level next. There is, however, one splendid fact which all aspirants should recognize: Mastery of the first level will lead, inevitably, to a competency in the second and, from the second, many, in humility and unawareness, will emerge into the third with some degree of creative proficiency and, thus, will be sought as tutors.

The way is not easy, but the reward for these achievements is individual liberty and, we submit, there is no other way.

• CHAPTER 12 •

CAN BUSY PEOPLE BECOME
LIBERTARIAN LEADERS?

A YOUNG BUSINESSMAN with whom I have a firsthand acquaintance has just begun a new and technical enterprise—from scratch and on a shoestring—straining all his energies and thoughts with only one end in view: getting his entrepreneurial duckling airborne. All other activities have been relegated to second place.

One other observation is relevant: This young man is a well-trained libertarian thinker, as accomplished as any businessman I know. With these facts in mind, it is understandable why he rebelled at a remark of mine: *"Every American is doing all he knows how to do on behalf of liberty."* Concluding that he was doing nothing on behalf of liberty, while solely preoccupied with his new enterprise, he took my remark to infer that he didn't know how to do anything. Mulling over his reaction, I came upon what to me is an important discovery and one which leads to the belief that this individual really is working on behalf of liberty in an effective manner. How? By employing what I choose to call "primary

knowledge." Not only does this man have *primary* knowledge to a marked degree but he practices it in every act
of his specialized occupation.

Anyway, it was this sequence of talk and retrospection
which led to a simple idea as to how our busiest people
can assist in rescuing liberty from her present plight.
They can do this without any more sacrifice of their
chosen work than it takes to learn the essential features
of primary knowledge and to get up the nerve to practice it—that is, to make it an integral part of their daily
occupations, whatever they happen to be. Let me explain.

Primary Knowledge

While not customarily so divided, knowledge can be
said to fall into two broad categories, primary and secondary. The nub of the idea under discussion is that
liberty depends exclusively on primary knowledge and
its practice, and not at all on secondary knowledge. If
this be a correct thought, then the path to liberty's rescue
lies in simple outline, even though it may be a rugged
path and call forth some difficult virtues to negotiate.

Primary knowledge, as the term suggests, is cognition
of the fundamental type or, more precisely, knowledge
of first importance. As hard to come by as some of it is,
it requires little in the way of expensive schools or knowledge factories. It is, in a sense, a universal or natural
knowledge which, when not realized, at least lies latent
in man and can be freed, more or less, by conscious

effort, the energizing of which is a strictly personal matter. The Law of Compensation is an instance: knowing that something dropped should be picked up; that a door opened should be closed; that a promise made should be kept; that money borrowed should be repaid; that with every right there is a responsibility. Other examples of primary knowledge:

> Knowing how little one knows, an essential quality of the nonauthoritarian: HUMILITY.
>
> Knowing of the rights of others, sometimes expressed as not doing unto others that which one would not have done unto self: JUSTICE.
>
> Knowing enough to count one's blessings—a riddance to envy, covetousness, political plunder: GRATITUDE.
>
> Knowing the importance of accurately reflecting that which one believes to be right: INTEGRITY.
>
> Knowing of a Consciousness over and beyond that of man (the rights to life and liberty are endowed by the Creator, not by the state): SPIRITUALITY.
>
> Knowing that one's own consciousness is expansible and knowing the high purpose of this unfolding or emerging or hatching process: AWARENESS.

Other Forms of Awareness

There are other forms of awareness that fall within the scope of primary knowledge. Awareness of danger is one. For example, were a person being held under water by another, he would struggle to free himself. Even animals have this instinctual type of knowledge.

But awareness or consciousness is on an inclining scale of its own. The loss of liberty, for instance, represents a danger much more difficult to discern than is the loss of oxygen which occasions drowning. The highly discerning person is aware that there can be no life where there are no liberties. Thus, fighting to retain liberty—a response to consciousness of danger—is tantamount to fighting for life itself, an action of first importance, an item far up the scale in the portfolio of primary knowledge.

Secondary Knowledge

Before commenting further on the relationship of primary knowledge to liberty, let's briefly consider the nature of secondary knowledge. This embraces all forms of specialized learning. Without this type of knowledge there would have been no advances in agriculture or industry or construction. There would be no engineers or architects or other specialists. We would have no clothing as we know it, no sanitary paraphernalia, no cars, planes, harvesters, tools, engines, electric power and light, and so on. Indeed, no more of us would be living in these United States than a foraging economy could support.[1]

But secondary knowledge, important as it is to life and to life extension, is actually a danger whenever we

---

[1] Estimating our present population at 182,000,000, at least 181,000,000 of us would not exist. The foraging American Indians, even with some agriculture, never numbered over 1,000,000, probably no more than 250,000.

become so preoccupied with it that we leave primary knowledge unattended. This is to say that whenever we become enamored of wealth and so busy piling up its numerous manifestations that we have neither the time nor the will for primary knowledge, nor the nerve to practice it, the whole wealth apparatus must crumble— as the Empire State Building would topple had it no foundation.

Dangers of Compulsory Methods

The dangers of secondary knowledge, in the absence of primary knowledge and its practice, are quite obvious, and examples of the danger are all about us. For instance, people who wish cheaper power and light and who do not possess such aspects of primary knowledge as humility and justice will employ the coercive powers of government to take the fruits of the labor of others to gratify their desire. There are other people, similarly deficient in primary knowledge, who will forcibly take the income of others as reimbursement for not growing tobacco (farm subsidy programs) or to renew their downtown business section (federal urban renewal) or to place three men on the moon (outer space program) or to satisfy their own charitable inclinations (government welfare programs) or—name something they won't do!

When we discuss how busy people can rescue liberty, we should stress the fact that it's *only* those who are capable of busying themselves who can give liberty a hand. The unbusy, the ones who merely seek entertainment, amusement, escape from life's problems, and self-indulgence can rarely be more than followers of whatever attracts them—not without changing their characters, an enormous undertaking.

This line of reasoning concludes that liberty is at the mercy of the practitioners of secondary knowledge, our busy specialists who, at the same time, possess primary knowledge. Liberty can't be saved by those who retire into their ivory towers or take to the hills, so to speak, to bemoan its plight.[2] It is the individual who is active who pushes liberty over the brink—or rescues her—depending on the nature of his actions. Inactive people are as uninfluential on this question as is any inert mass.

Liberty Comes with Living

Is it not apparent that liberty depends exclusively on primary knowledge and its practice, and not at all on secondary knowledge? Liberty is not helped or harmed by knowledge of a mathematical formula or how to raise beef or bake bread or repair a motor. But dispense with justice, integrity, and other primary virtues, and liberty cannot exist. This is self-evident. So, there is no suggestion here that any person retire from or even diminish his activity in any honorable, specialized occupation. This is not a question of *either* specializing *or* rescuing

---

[2] This is only to frown on a withdrawal from life's problems, not to belittle reflection and contemplation.

liberty. Actually, it is a matter of doing both at the same time.

We have here the most important problem of integration there is—integrating primary knowledge with specialized practice, and on the part of busy people. Little more is required than a strict observance of the disciplines which primary knowledge supplies. Extend division of labor to the heart's content as long as the specialized activities are within the framework of such virtues as integrity, willing exchange, and the rights of others. This will leave no loopholes to support or sponsor any of the legalized immoralities so rampant in our time.

No shoemaker would stick to his last were his shop burning down. He would try to put out the fire in order that he might again stick to his last. Aware persons know that their specialized busy-ness has no future except as liberty prevails. If each busy individual, in all his countless actions, would take no action except as it strictly accords with the axioms implicit in primary knowledge, that individual would be serving liberty persuasively and influentially. Radiating rightness is what this amounts to!

Every American is doing all he knows how to do on behalf of liberty. Does he know enough? If this thesis be correct, the answer ought to come quickly and clearly to any person who will ask himself the question.

• CHAPTER 13 •

LIBERATED!

"How LONG have you been interested in this philosophy?" I asked the graduate student in education, who wanted to learn more about the subject of freedom.

Her response struck me as sensational in the clarity of what it revealed: "I have now been *liberated* for six months." This conjures up a picture of a person imprisoned by a host of myths, superstitions, fallacies. Then, in a flash, by some unforeseen encounter, she was freed of them all and launched on a new road to enlightenment. Liberation, as she used the term, suggested a sudden illumination, a break-through to a higher level of consciousness: "Whereas I was blind, now I see."

It is interesting to reflect on the preliberation notions. In many cases we find lying at their root the primitive doctrine that man derives his rights to life and liberty from some man-concocted collective—the tribe or the state. This doctrine was frankly expressed in the old divine-right-of-kings thesis, an egotism few present-day statists have the nerve to admit.

The logical sequence to such a premise is the conviction that the state is responsible for a people's welfare,

176

security, prosperity. And if the state can grant a man's rights, it can also retract them; that is, it is in control of rights. Freedom of choice as to how one employs himself or what he does with the fruits of his own labor is expanded or contracted according to the caprice of those who have gained command of the political apparatus. Wage and price controls, government education, public housing, federal urban renewal, government power and light, socialized medicine, government mail delivery, social security, federal subsidies to any and all groups who think themselves in distress, protection against competition, progressive taxation, and a host of other socializations or nationalizations are simply extensions of the premise that man's rights derive from the state.

The Break-Through

Out of this confusion emerges an intensely personal experience—the moment of liberation, the break-through! An idea or fact or observation, germinating in the mind for an indeterminate period, suddenly comes to life, opens a crack, and the light floods in. It's something like a seed embedded in a crevice of solid granite, the forces of its growth slumbering but, when released, stronger than its rock-bound prison. Its destiny undeniable, the seed splits the stone and is freed to friendly and life-giving elements.[1]

Once this opening has taken place, old ideas take on

---

[1] For instance, *Betula Nigra,* sometimes known as "The Rock Splitting Birch."

a different perspective and new ideas come into one's comprehension. Relegated to the junk heap of myths is the absurd premise that man derives his rights from a political apparatus. To the question, "How could man, who knows next to nothing about himself, create himself or preside over creation?" comes a resounding "Impossible!" Rid of this bedeviling notion, a new premise insinuates itself into consciousness: Men are endowed by their Creator with certain inalienable rights, among them the right to life, liberty, and the pursuit of happiness. Or, as Bastiat later put it:

> We hold from God the gift which includes all others. This gift is life—physical, intellectual, and moral life.
>
> But life cannot maintain itself alone. The Creator of life has entrusted us with the responsibility of preserving, developing, and perfecting it. In order that we may accomplish this, He has provided us with a collection of marvelous faculties. And He has put us in the midst of a variety of natural resources. By the application of our faculties to these natural resources we convert them into products, and use them. This process is necessary in order that life may run its appointed course.
>
> Life, faculties, production—in other words, individuality, liberty, property—this is man. And in spite of the cunning of artful political leaders, these three gifts from God precede all human legislation, and are superior to it.
>
> Life, liberty, and property do not exist because men have made laws. On the contrary, it was the fact that life, liberty, and property existed beforehand that caused men to make laws in the first place.[2]

---

[2] Frederic Bastiat, *The Law*, translated by Dean Russell (Irvington-on-Hudson, N. Y.: The Foundation for Economic Education, Inc., 1950), pp. 5-6.

The Creator-Man Relationship

One logical deduction from the premise that man's rights are endowments of the Creator is that each individual is an end in himself, that is, each person owes allegiance, above all else, to his Creator. No other person or set of persons, however organized, has any moral sanction to interfere with this Creator-man relationship; no person is warranted in compelling any human being to serve merely as a means to his own ends. When anyone violates this relationship, he is saying, in effect, "*I* am your god."

It follows from the above premise that man-made laws can be no more than codified social taboos or a set of prohibitions, for the purpose of preserving inviolate the Creator-man order. All true law finds its origin and its limitation in such rights of protection as inhere in each of us. How can we tell what these rights are? Merely ascertain if universality can be applied to them. Do I, for example, have a right to defend my life, livelihood, liberty against those who would take these from me? Only if the same right may rationally be conceded to everyone else. Can it be? Obviously, yes! Now, then, do I have a right to take the life, livelihood, liberty of another? Only if the right of murder, theft, slavery may rationally be conceded to everyone else. Can it be? Obviously, no!

It follows logically from this premise that government may properly do no more than perform the defensive function. All productive and creative actions are then freed of any man-restraint, flowing solely from the Cre-ator-man order.

When an individual is liberated, he becomes aware of the miracles which come to pass once creative human energy has no organized, man-concocted force standing against it. An unwavering faith in free men expels any lingering, misplaced confidence in little men playing god.

The omnipotent state—authoritarianism—will not be liquidated except by liberated individuals. It is only they who go in search of freedom's answers. Until the time of liberation, they are no more teachable than a parakeet; they can repeat what they read or hear but they cannot *know.* If only liberated individuals can be of any help in reversing the trend away from freedom, it is impor-tant to take note of what brings about liberation.

No Master Key

Experience reveals no master key. Each mind has a unique lock. The keys presently in our possession may or may not fit. Said the student, "I have now been *liber-ated* for six months." I made inquiry of her mentor, "What did you say to cause the break-through?" In this instance it had to do with self-responsibility, pointing out that the state can no more assume the responsibility for one's welfare, security, prosperity than can a com-mittee of baboons. Indeed, the responsibility for self is no more transferable than is breathing. Yet, people can be lulled into this false notion and, as a consequence, forego attention to self-responsibility, becoming purposeless and useless. But, unfortunately, this key will not fit the lock to most unopened minds.

One brilliant libertarian thinker confessed that he had been a socialist in high school, that a friend tirelessly labored with him until, finally, he saw the light. "What key did he use to unlock your mind?" I asked.

"George came to my home for dinner. I was showing him our new refrigerator. He asked me how I would allocate refrigerators, were it not for the price system. It was this recognition of the free market's allocation of scarce resources that triggered the change in me."

An outstanding worker for liberty acknowledged that he had finished college as a socialist. What proved to be the key to his mind? It was "Why the Worst Get on Top," a chapter in Hayek's *The Road to Serfdom*.[3]

A Wichita business leader was liberated by an idea in Weaver's *Mainspring*.[4] How varied the keys!

Those who have been liberated can and do help one another—the educable aiding the educable! That we need more liberated individuals is self-evident; for among the non-liberated are, unquestionably, some of the greatest potential writers, thinkers, talkers of the

---

[3] F. A. Hayek, *The Road to Serfdom* (Chicago: The University of Chicago Press, 1944).

[4] Henry Grady Weaver, *The Mainspring of Human Progress* (Irvington-on-Hudson, N. Y.: The Foundation for Economic Education, Inc., 1953).

freedom philosophy. But what can any of us do about
it? How can we liberate them?

At the outset, it might be well to consider some of
our limitations. The individual not yet liberated is no
more educable as to the free market, private property,
limited government philosophy than you or I are educable on subjects in which we have no interest. Thus, it
is patently absurd to scold or rant at them, to be impa-
tient, to regard them as not bright, to try poking our
ideas down their necks. Such tactics will only send them
scurrying.

Patience Pays Dividends

The best counsel is to take it easy. First, we must recognize that most of the individuals among our personal
contacts—be they ditch diggers or Ph.D.'s—have no aptitudes whatever for this subject. Might as well practice
our wiles at the zoo!

Work naturally; make freely available such insights
as you possess, but do not entertain any notions about
setting someone else straight. Go only where called, *but
qualify to be called.* The few within your orbit who are
susceptible to the freedom philosophy will find you out.
We need never worry about that, only about our own
qualifications. In this manner we will liberate as many
minds as will open to our own keys.

One example of exploration: Many of my hours are
spent in air travel. Is my seat companion a socialist or
what? Striking up a conversation is easy enough. And

just as easy is to converse in such a manner that he or she cannot help asking, within a few minutes, "What, pray tell, do *you* do?" His or her reaction to my brief answer will instantly reveal to me whether or not he or she has any interest in freedom. If negative, I return to my reading or writing; if affirmative, I'll have a new worker in the vineyard when the plane touches down at Idlewild or wherever.

This unobtrusive type of exploration lends itself to any number of adaptations. It is productive as well as good exercise. Further, it is fun. Have a try at it. You may liberate someone. If you do, count on it, you'll have made one of the best friends, ever. And you will have struck another blow for freedom!

CPSIA information can be obtained
at www.ICGtesting.com
Printed in the USA
LVHW011940130121
676409LV00042B/698

9 781258 396190